Authentic

HOW TO BE YOURSELF
& WHY IT MATTERS

Professor
Stephen Joseph

piatkus

PIATKUS

First published in Great Britain in 2016 by Piatkus

1 3 5 7 9 10 8 6 4 2

The illustration on page 138 is reproduced with
the kind permission of Kristin Neff.
The names of individuals featured in this book have
been changed to protect their privacy.

A CIP catalogue record for this book
is available from the British Library.

ISBN 978-0-349-40484-4

Typeset in Miller Text by M Rules
Printed and bound in Great Britain by
Clays Ltd, St Ives plc

Papers used by Piatkus are from well-managed forests
and other responsible sources.

MIX
Paper from
responsible sources
FSC
www.fsc.org   FSC® C104740

Piatkus
An imprint of
Little, Brown Book Group
Carmelite House
50 Victoria Embankment
London EC4Y 0DZ

An Hachette UK Company
www.hachette.co.uk

www.improvementzone.co.uk

Psychologist Stephen Joseph, PhD, is interested in the study of human flourishing. Known internationally as a leading expert in positive psychology, he is the editor of the ground-breaking book *Positive Psychology in Practice: Promoting human flourishing in work, health, education and everyday life.*

He studied at the London School of Economics, before going on to gain his doctorate from King's College London Institute of Psychiatry, Psychology and Neuroscience for his pioneering work in the field of psychological trauma. His previous book *What Doesn't Kill Us: A guide to overcoming adversity and moving forward* is available in translation across the world.

A coaching psychologist whose focus is on applying ideas from positive psychology, he helps people overcome challenges and find authentic, new directions in their personal and professional lives.

www.authenticityformula.com

In memory of Carl R. Rogers (1902–1987),
who showed us that it is in good relationships
that we are most able to be ourselves

Contents

Acknowledgements

There are a number of scholars whose work has influenced me greatly, but I am particularly grateful for the work of Abraham Maslow and Carl Rogers. Sadly no longer with us, they are remembered for their important writings and research in humanistic psychology.

More recent scholars I am indebted to, who have provided new research insights, include Edward Deci, Veronika Huta, Tim Kasser, Kristin Neff, Richard Ryan and Ken Sheldon. My thanks to them and to the many others whose research I have mentioned throughout and in the notes at the end of the book.

My thanks also to Michael Baliousis, Alex Linley, John Maltby and Alex Wood, the original team who developed the Authenticity Scale with me. I am grateful for their collaborations. Without their expertise in data collection and statistical testing, the project could not have been developed as successfully as it did.

Writing this book has been a passion of mine, and I would like to thank my agent Peter Tallack who stuck with me throughout the initial proposal stages and helped me shape my vision for the book. Thanks also to my editor Anne Lawrance, at Little, Brown, for her encouragement, support, confidence in me, and for taking the book to the next stage. And thanks also to Jillian Stewart, my project editor at Little, Brown, who oversaw the final stages of production, and to Jan Cutler for her skilful and helpful copyediting.

Most of all I want to thank the many people whose stories I have told in this book, many of whom I have had the privilege to work with over the years as clients in counselling or coaching, but who remain anonymous, and also the hundreds of people who have taken part in my research studies over the years, and to the participants of the many other research projects mentioned in the book. It is only through the willingness of so many to take part in experiments, surveys and interviews that we know what we do.

My thanks to friends and colleagues who let me bounce ideas around and commented on earlier drafts of chapters. Thanks especially to Sian Clifford for her inspiration and encouragement. Others whose support has also been helpful are Saul Becker, Liz Blakey, Laura Blackie, David Browne, Lindsay Cooper, Mick Cooper, Zoë Chouliara, Kate Hayes, Nicki Hitchcott, Rob Hooper, Chris Lewis, Lynne McCormack, David Murphy, Steve Regel, Christian van Nieuwerburgh and Pete Wilkins. Finally, my thanks to Vanessa Markey for her unwavering support, love and friendship over many years.

To Thine Own Self Be True

The above title is a quote from Shakespeare's *Hamlet*, where Polonius encourages his son, Laertes, to live a full life without self-deception.[1] Throughout the ages, philosophers and other scholars have speculated on what it means to be oneself and to live a life that is true to that self. Surprisingly, it is only within the last decade that psychologists have begun to sit up and take notice of this sage advice and to subject it to scrutiny.[2]

It was in the 1990s when I was studying to become a psychotherapist that I first encountered the notion of authenticity through the work of the late, great Carl Rogers. Rogers was one of the most influential psychotherapists and psychologists of the 20th century. For Rogers, authenticity meant being the author of one's own life. He saw this as a difficult process of always striving for balance in the process of realising one's own needs, while living together with others in such a way that meets the needs of those relationships. As such, authenticity required the person to understand themselves, to have awareness of their inner emotional states and to possess the ability to be openly expressive of these states with others. For Rogers, it was the ability of people to live in such a 'congruent' way that made for the 'good life' – by which he meant living more purposefully and meaningfully, and seeking ever greater authenticity in each and every moment.

As a psychotherapist, Rogers believed that people seeking help were most often characterised by a lack of authenticity in their lives. In his view, experiences of distress were often an expression that one was out of balance, and a cry for help to become more authentic.[3]

To help people live more authentic lives, Rogers developed a form of psychotherapy known as 'client-centred therapy'. This was based on the idea that when people feel truly accepted for who they are, they don't feel the need to put on a façade. Instead of pretending to themselves and to others that they are something they are not, they start listening to their own inner voice of wisdom and begin to make more authentic decisions about how to lead their lives. As they become more authentic in themselves and with other people, their lives take on new direction, meaning and purpose.[4]

In my other role as a university teacher of psychology, I was intrigued by these ideas of Carl Rogers, but surprised at how little research there was. Sadly, since his death in 1987, the depth and detail of his ideas had begun to be forgotten by the modern generation of psychologists. At least, that was the case before the positive psychologists came along and made the study of the good life fashionable and began to look back at these earlier ideas.

Previously, most psychologists were interested only in the dark side of people's lives – depression, anxiety and all the other ways in which lives become blighted. For most, well-being meant the absence of problems of depression, anxiety and so on. Only a handful of us were interested in going beyond what I called this zero point to understand the presence of states of happiness and contentment.[5]

At the time I was developing my interest in these earlier ideas of Carl Rogers, a brilliant new student came to work with me. Alex Linley had just completed his psychology degree. He enrolled with me to study for his PhD.[6] Alex was passionate about the positive psychology that was, by then, just emerging and beginning to attract wider interest among scholars. He could see the potential in the idea of authenticity. We wanted to know if we could find a way to measure authenticity and whether it was indeed the road to a happy and fulfilled life. Together we drew up a list of questions that we thought were important to ask. Later, with the collaboration of other students and colleagues, Alex Wood, John Maltby and Michael Baliousis, we went on to develop the first psychometric test based on Carl Rogers's theory of authenticity – the Authenticity Scale.[7]

Interested in whether more authentic people were happier, we found that when compared with a range of other personality factors, authenticity came out top as the factor that most readily distinguishes happy from unhappy people. Now used across the world by many researchers and psychologists, the Authenticity Scale helped pave the way for the new science of authenticity, which is showing us that living an authentic life may indeed be the surest road to lasting fulfilment.

It wasn't only in the sterile world of our laboratory research that I began to understand the importance of authenticity, however. By now I had moved to a new position as co-director of the Centre for Trauma, Resilience and Growth where, with my colleague Steve Regel, we were interested in understanding the remarkable transformations in people who have confronted trauma and adversity. Most of our patients were suffering from post-traumatic stress, but, intriguingly, we also observed that many talked about how their close encounter with death had awoken them to new possibilities in life and enabled them to find new strengths within themselves. Positive psychologists now have a term for such changes in survivors of trauma: post-traumatic growth.[8] As I began to understand more about post-traumatic growth, it was clear to me that the common thread for all survivors was their new desire to live in a way that was more true to themselves. What seemed most characteristic of post-traumatic growth was how it brought about a retelling of a person's life story and its alignment with their goals and values, creating greater coherence in their lives. To me, it seemed that post-traumatic growth was really about how the experience of adversity acts like a catalyst for people's desire to live more authentically.[9]

Striving for authenticity does not mean a life free from pain, fear, grief or sorrow, but it allows us to live more purposefully and meaningfully, especially when confronted by suffering. Trauma teaches the lesson that life is short and precious and that it is therefore wise to live it to the full, in ways that involve shifting priorities towards what really matters. If we are fortunate, we will go through our lives without encountering traumas, but often the downside of a life free from adversity is that we sleepwalk through our lives without a wake-up call to remind us about what is important. It seems tragic that so many of us have to wait until confronted by our own or a loved one's mortality before we wake up to the understanding that we have focused on the wrong things. Only then, in the light of tragedy and loss, do we appreciate what we had and begin to change our lives so that they are more authentic.

I was curious about how best to communicate the wisdom of trauma survivors to my other patients. Do we have to wait for tragedy to strike before we can learn this most valuable lesson? Or can we simply choose right now to walk down the road of authenticity? What I have learned is that we can. If we choose, we can learn from the wisdom of others and make it our task to wake up to what really matters – an authentic life.

Research by Bronnie Ware, an Australian palliative nurse, found that the most common regret of those about to die was not having had the courage to live a life true to oneself.[10] I saw this myself quite recently following my father's diagnosis of cancer. Frail and confined to bed, one afternoon he looked over at me and said: 'I spent my life worrying about things that don't matter. Make sure you enjoy yourself; it all goes very quickly.' A few days later, his condition deteriorated and he was carried out of the house by the paramedics. As they lifted him through the front door for the last time I remember that he sighed with some pleasure as he breathed in the fresh autumn air for the first time in weeks.

At my father's funeral I recalled how he always said that he would have liked to have been a saxophone player. He loved jazz music. But he had spent his life working in a job that he said he detested. The funeral wasn't a religious service, so in my eulogy I was able to ask those in attendance to imagine that in some way, in some basement jazz club somewhere, a new saxophonist would be taking to the stage. It is comforting to imagine that those we are close to somehow carry on in ways that allow them to be more true to themselves than they managed to be in their lives.

What I have come to realise is that the longing to lead an authentic life is the common theme of people seeking help. I meet many people who wish that they had made different choices in their lives, such as living somewhere else, choosing a different career, or marrying someone other than their current partner. Often such thoughts become all-consuming for the person seeking help, as they ponder whether it is too late for them to make such changes. The distress caused by living a life that is not true to oneself lies at the heart of many of the problems that psychotherapists and psychologists encounter in their clinics. But it is not only those seeking help who quest for authenticity – we all do.

We all think about the shape our lives have taken and may wonder what new directions to go in. The choices we make in life boil down to what matters to us at the time. This can change. Someone who puts their career above all else finds him- or

herself later in life realising that they lack strong personal relationships. Someone else who has prioritised their relationship
finds that they feel they missed out on a career.

Choosing wisely about what matters to you is vital to all
aspects of your life: your well-being, the success of your relationships, how your career unfolds and how you look back on your
own life. As I will show in this book, to choose wisely requires
that you know yourself, own yourself and be yourself, from
moment to moment. This is the formula for authentic living.

In all of our interactions in life, whether it is between parents and
children, teachers and students, employers and their employees,
work colleagues, friends or sexual partners, the most important
aspect is authenticity and the ability to communicate clearly
about what matters to us. What I have to say about authenticity derives from the wisdom of the ancient Greek philosopher
Aristotle, the ideas of the humanistic psychologists of the mid-
20th century, such as Carl Rogers and Abraham Maslow, and
the scientific work of modern-day positive psychologists.

Specifically, the good human life requires that we fulfil the
potentials inherent in our nature. Each of us has our own
unique mix of character strengths, abilities and talents. Like a
plant that receives just the right amount of water and sunlight,
we too will flourish if our basic needs are correctly nurtured.
This is not to say that there is some predestined plan for each
of us, but that if our basic needs are met, we will be free to
grow and develop to become the best version of ourselves that
we can be.

The more we are able to be ourselves, the happier we will
be. And the happier we are, the more we contribute to the bet-
terment of those around us. However, if our potentialities go
unfulfilled, the more distressed, damaged and dysfunctional
we become and the greater we contribute to the destructive
forces in the world. Not all psychological problems can be

linked to a lack of authenticity in our lives but a lot, and perhaps most, can.

One of the questions that people ask when they first meet me and learn that I work as a psychotherapist and psychologist is how I deal with listening to other people's stories of distress. At times it can be difficult but, more often, such work adds to my own vitality and determination to live my own life in an authentic and meaningful way.[11] What I have learned from my clients is that it is possible to turn our lives around right now, if we so choose.

I have been inspired in my own life, by my clients and from my research, to seek a more authentic life. I hope this book will inspire you.

How to use this book

Authenticity has recently become a popular topic among positive psychologists, who have come to realise that it is no soft option but the cornerstone of a good life. I will put the study of authenticity into the context of recent scientific developments in positive psychology.

Along the way, we will look at the defences and distortions that we use to prop up our inauthentic lives and avoid confronting the truth about ourselves. If it is hard to pin down what authenticity is, it is easier to see what it isn't. When we are defensive, we are by definition not authentic. By beginning to understand our patterns of defence, we can learn to be the authors of our own lives.

Reading the book may well prompt you towards wanting to be more authentic in your own life. If so, you'll find exercises to try. These are designed to trigger your thoughts about yourself and to offer you some guidance that may help. Throughout, I have included case-study excerpts. These are based on real people, but the details are sufficiently disguised so that they remain anonymous. Also, some cases are a blend of more than one person's story.

See it as the start of a new adventure, take the exercises seriously and think long and hard about the questions asked. You may find it helpful to have a notebook to hand for some of the exercises and to make a record of your observations. I find it is often helpful to write the answers down, because when we write we stay focused on what we are doing. When we sit and think about something, our mind wanders and we lose our train of thought. Writing it down keeps us on track and provides a record of thoughts we might otherwise forget. Recording any thoughts and feelings that come to you can also be a powerful way of helping you notice consistent themes and ideas.

A book like this can offer only so much, but if it serves to kick-start positive change in your life, then I will be content that it has done its job.

Chapter 1

The Authenticity Formula

Often, it is significant birthdays that cause us to reflect on our life journey: typically, it is as we approach the milestone ages such as 30, 40, 50 or 60 years that we look back over the previous decades and wonder at how we have arrived where we have, perhaps so distant from the dreams of our younger selves. We might fantasise about changing career, leaving our partners, travelling the world or whatever, to find a new and more fulfilling life, but few of us ever act upon such fantasies.

More likely, you are sitting at your desk at work, when your boss appears over your shoulder and asks you to prepare some figures for the meeting tomorrow. Your heart sinks. You had already told him that the figures weren't ready yet, but he sounds tense, and you know from past experience that it is not the time to argue with him. Once he gets something in his mind, there is no use arguing – you know you now have to cancel your plans for the evening and get the figures prepared as best you can. Sitting on the train on the way home you wonder what has become of your life and the hopes you once had. What happened to those dreams of becoming an architect, an artist, a fashion designer, writing a novel, cycling the Tour de France, playing the flute, or whatever it might be?

Sitting on the train, in that moment, you know that you have a choice: to carry on with your life as it is or to begin to make a change. But what would that change look like? Do you, as in the story above, fantasise about disappearing into a new life? Does a sense of reality then creep up on you as you think to yourself: *How would I manage to do this? Would I earn enough money to live on? What about the children's futures?* The challenge to turn your life around is simply too great. Perhaps you pick up a magazine and lose yourself in stories of the latest celebrity scandal or the sports pages of the newspaper, or perhaps you pour a glass of wine and settle back to watch a favourite television series.

Sometimes, though, just sometimes, people don't pick up the magazine, or switch on the television, or pour a glass of wine. Something clicks into place. The decision is made to do things differently. You may not know yet what changes you want to make, only that you don't want to carry on exactly as you are. As a psychologist, the thing I hear most often from people is their longing in some way or other to be more true to themselves.

What I've discovered is this: people get stuck because they think that to be true to themselves they must know, right now, what their longer-term goals are and be able to see clearly the steps they need to take in order to achieve them. And so, if they don't know exactly what it will mean to be more true to themselves in the longer term, they do nothing. The truth, however, as I've discovered, is that you don't need to know what your longer-term goals are to begin leading a life that is true to yourself. Being true to yourself is about what you do, think and feel, right now in this moment. Then, as your life unfolds day by day, you begin to see, more clearly, the road ahead open up in front of you.

It is by travelling along the right roads for you that you can lead a fulfilling, rewarding and enjoyable life.

The struggle to find your own true path

As a counsellor and coach, I have worked with people of varying ages and backgrounds but, below the surface of their different problems, there is often a common thread to their stories, and that is the struggle to find their own authentic path in life.

CASE STUDY: *Sarah*

Sarah is in her forties, having had a very successful career. She is a senior executive working for a large national company. On the whole, she does not dislike her work, but at the same time she feels that she is not fulfilling her potential. In the mornings she has no excitement for the day ahead. She longs for a career in which she feels like she would be stretching herself to learn and develop in new ways, and using more of her experiences and what she is good at. She gets along well enough with her colleagues but she doesn't particularly like any of them or count them as friends. She yearns to be among people she values and who inspire her to new heights. She desires to be more creative and autonomous; to be able to make a difference in people's lives and to feel more alive herself.

She also feels stuck in her career and is seeking a new direction. In her personal life she has recently decided to divorce her husband.

In our first session, she told me about the day 20 years previously when her then boyfriend proposed to her. 'Will you marry me?' he asked. Without thinking, she immediately replied, 'No.' Then, as she saw the crestfallen look on his face, she added, 'Of course I will.' Her gut reaction was to say no but, overcome by her need to please, she said yes. And that set the course of her life for the next 20 years. As she told me this story, tears welled up in her eyes. We sat in silence for a few minutes taking in the enormity of the consequences of this single moment 20 years previously and how it had set her on the road that had taken her to this point in her life.

In a later session, Sarah was explaining to me that she wasn't happy and was looking for more fulfilment and enjoyment from life. She discussed her options with me and the pros and cons of each as they seemed to her. She certainly seemed to know what she didn't want, but she was less sure of what she did want. After almost an hour she asked me, 'What should I do?'

'I don't know what you should do. It is a big decision, but in the end it is you that has to make it,' I replied. Sarah looked at me and I could tell she was getting frustrated. Here we were after several sessions having the same conversation again. I knew from a previous conversation that Sarah had the unrealistic expectation of coaching that she would leave with all her problems solved and the perfect plan for her future.

'It takes time to work these things out,' I said. Sarah looked at me and I thought she was probably wondering what she was paying me for. 'There is no finishing line beyond which you can sit back and say, "I'm happy now and that's the way it is from here on in",' I said, beginning to wonder myself what she was paying me for. But then I could see a light-bulb moment happen for her as her eyes lit up and she looked straight at me. Encouraged, I remembered the first session and I said, 'It's like when you agreed to get married; in that moment you set the direction of your life, but the direction came from your need to please your boyfriend, not from within you and your inner wisdom of what was right for you. Every day is full of such moments, requiring us to make a decision. You might not have known exactly what you wanted at that point, but you did know you didn't want to say yes. You wanted to say no. If we are true to ourselves as much as we can be in each and every moment and trust our inner voice of wisdom, the more the new direction of our lives will become clear. It's a bit like being in a boat and making small tilts of the rudder that eventually take you to a new destination, miles from the course you were originally on.'

Sarah left the session that day not with a plan for how the rest of her life should be but with little goals for the next few days. The main one was to be more true to herself in an upcoming meeting with a potential colleague. The colleague was someone she didn't enjoy working with but who had asked her to be part of a new venture. Sarah's initial gut reaction was to say no but she had said yes, because, just like she had done 20 years ago with her then boyfriend, she wanted to please. But with the realisation that it is in these single small moments that our lives are shaped, she knew that she had to go back to her colleague and now say no to the request. She still didn't know for certain what direction she wanted her life to go in, but she was beginning to take a stronger grip on the rudder of her own life and to make sure she didn't take the wrong direction this time.

The small parts of life are so important

Authenticity is about being true to yourself in each and every moment. Sarah's story illustrates so well how it is those small decisions of everyday life that shape the big directions that we take. As you read Sarah's story about how she went against her gut feelings and agreed to get married, you might recall a similar moment from your own life – perhaps when you went against your own gut feelings – and which you now look back upon as pivotal.

When we reflect on our past, we can see that the directions we have taken can often be traced back to one single, short moment. Our lives often turn on what at the time seem to be the most trivial of occurrences: a chance meeting and a single sentence that was or wasn't said. As one ages and becomes wiser, it becomes possible to see that life is governed in this way and that the big things in life, such as who one marries, what career one pursues, where one lives and so on, often arise from such unexpected everyday and, at the time, seemingly trivial encounters. To be able to navigate life successfully, so that you make the best decisions for yourself at any given moment, you need to be authentic – you need to be able to counter external influences pulling you to go against the grain of your own gut feelings. Authenticity is at the heart of our decision-making and it is in each and every small moment in life that it makes a difference. We are constantly in the process of creating ourselves.

In hindsight, it is possible to see what the pivotal points of our life have been. But this is not about looking back with regret; rather, it is about learning to live authentically in each and every moment.

The psychological tension of inauthenticity

From when we wake up in the morning to when we go to sleep, most of us have at least some points in our day when we can be truly ourselves, but for many parts of the day we are putting on a show. For good reason, we do not say or show what we truly think or feel.

We put on a façade that everything is going well. We feel

pressure to present ourselves positively to others, whether it is in a passing greeting on the street, in the office or on social media sites, as leading a happy life.

'How are you?'

'Good,' we automatically reply, no matter what is going on in our lives.

Take, as another example, the place where we spend most of our time: work. Many workplaces are rife with seething resentments, bitterness and conflicts that rarely get expressed. We all know that it is often better to hold our tongue. We might be frightened of losing our jobs, or of being gossiped about or losing friends; whatever the reason for many of us, much of our waking lives involves walking on eggshells around others, biting our tongue or smiling when we feel irritated or angry.

Those of us who work with others, particularly dealing face to face with customers day after day, know all too well the pressures of keeping up a friendly smile. A recent report described how staff at a company in Japan were allowed a day when they could wear expressionless 'no-face' masks to work to reduce the pressure on them and help them relax after spending a year smiling at customers.[1] Simply put, living an inauthentic life can be exhausting.

Consider a typical case.

CASE STUDY: *Pam*

Pam couldn't sleep. She was furious with her boss, Dennis. He had lied to her about a project and left her in a situation in which she was about to get the blame for something that wasn't her fault. Unless she could transform the fortunes of the project by the time of the meeting the next day, her job would be in jeopardy. Pam had considered Dennis a good friend, but no longer. She got to work early. Walking down the corridor, she saw

him coming towards her. As they passed, they smiled
and said good morning as if nothing had happened. Only
then did she think to herself how duplicitous he was and
how slow she had been to realise this. She had learned a
lesson but was wise enough, for the time being, to keep
her thoughts to herself.

There are times and places when it may be appropriate
to keep our thoughts to ourselves. Pam knew exactly what
she was doing and why. As frustrated as she was, she
knew that it would not benefit her to express her anger
that day to that person, and that doing so might even
jeopardise her career. She decided to keep her thoughts to
herself and try to mask her inner anger with an outer smile.

Living inauthentically – wearing a mask

One of my favourite quotes, often attributed to Dr Seuss, is,
'Be who you are and say what you feel because those who mind
don't matter and those who matter don't mind.'[2] As a broad
generalisation, this is helpful, but there are exceptions, because
sometimes those who mind *do* matter, in terms of having real
power over you that could be used maliciously. It is a useful
social skill to be able to mask your authentic feelings, and there
are times and places when that will be the wisest thing to do. It
is up to each of us to judge when that is.

Living inauthentically, however, when what we say and do
does not match how we think and feel, creates an inner psychological tension that can be distressing.[3] If we live inauthentically,
day after day, it is likely to take an emotional toll on us.

Low levels of well-being and even depression and anxiety, may
result when we attempt to live a life that is misaligned between
our sense of self and the reality of our situation (see Appendix I
to test your own level of well-being).

To ease the distress, we wish to create harmony between what is going on inside us with what we express. In an ideal life, what we say and do would be consistent with what we think and feel. Pam wants to be able to be more genuine in her expression, and her hope is that her relationships at work will change in such a way that that is possible. But there is also the danger that eventually, if she continues to put on a façade in public, she will change within herself in such a way that, as the social psychologist Erving Goffman put it, her mask becomes her face.[4] Pam might find there is a psychological price to pay if she does not find a way to end the tension, but for now she is making the best choice she can, which is to smile through gritted teeth in full awareness of what she is doing.

Like Pam, you might feel you are wearing a mask to cover your true feelings. Many people feel as if they do, but are frightened to remove their mask.

Be aware of your whole body

Knowing that things do not feel right is one thing, but making changes in our lives can be difficult. It takes courage to face up to ourselves, humility to accept what we learn about ourselves and discipline to take action. As such, it might feel safer to drift along and settle for things as they are. Many of us live our lives waiting for something to happen that will change our situation. We continue to live inauthentically. We become numb to the mental discomfort and physical tension that we carry.

Even as you read this, you might now feel the tension in your neck, in your shoulders or in your forehead simply because I have drawn your attention to it. Take a few moments and be aware of the tension in your jaw. Release some of that tension with a yawn. Now stretch your shoulders back, hold that for a second and then release. Clench and unclench your toes; do it again. Feeling a bit better?

Authenticity requires that we are aware of what's happening in our bodies; that we are not only attentive to our feelings and mindful of our thinking but to all that is happening within us. Instead, many of us experience ourselves as minds sitting on top of our bodies, as if we were riding a horse. Much of the time we are unaware of our body, but every so often we need to feed and clean it and sometimes urge it on with the whip.[5] But we are not disembodied minds, we are our bodies. We need to be able to listen to ourselves to be fully aware of what is going on within us – all our feelings, thoughts and physical sensations.

Listen to your inner voice

One of the most influential entrepreneurs of the last decades was Steve Jobs, who died in October 2011. In an address to students graduating from Stanford University he said:

> Your time is limited, so don't waste it living someone else's life. Don't be trapped by dogma – which is living with the results of other people's thinking. Don't let the noise of others' opinions drown out your own inner voice. And, most important, have the courage to follow your heart and intuition. They somehow already know what you truly want to become. Everything else is secondary.[6]

The quote from Steve Jobs sums up pretty well what I mean by authenticity.

By inner voice, I don't mean the relentless mental chatter of self-criticism and rumination that many of us live with, particularly in the small hours of the night when we can't stop worrying about a meeting the next day, what was said the day before, the bills that need to be paid, an argument with a friend or relative, or whatever it might be that keeps us awake at night. We have to learn how to block out all that mental noise and strain to hear our own inner voice of wisdom. At first, our own inner voice might be only a faint whisper, as we begin to realise that behind the inner gremlins there is another voice that belongs to us. By listening carefully we can begin to trust that voice to be our reliable compass point.

It seems to me that the importance of being true to yourself is a lesson that most of us learn sooner or later. Certainly, I wish I had learned sooner in my own life to be more aware of my own inner voice of wisdom. And I am still learning, day by day, to be more attentive to it. Authenticity is not an end point so that once it is achieved you can sit back and relax; rather, it is an ongoing process whereby we constantly need to be attentive to our inner world and how we experience ourselves, moment by moment.

We will return to the steps we can take to develop our abilities to listen to ourselves later in the book, but for now I want to say that Steve Jobs's words are probably the best advice anyone can ever heed for how to live their life. Steve Jobs may not have known it, but his words echo the best thinking today among positive psychologists about how to live a good life and what it means to be authentic.

In the following pages I will introduce you to the authenticity formula, but first we will consider the three things that authentic people do.

The three things that authentic people do

To summarise, there are three things that authentic people do well: they know themselves, they own themselves and they are prepared to be themselves.

Know yourself

Authentic people know what they like and what they dislike, what they are good at and what they are less good at, what they are prepared to do and what they aren't prepared to do. They are able to be present in the moment, aware of what is going on inside them emotionally and of what is happening around them, and they are able to take in what is happening for what it is. They are able to notice without labelling or judging.

To be authentic, we need to be able to face up to the truth about ourselves, no matter how unpleasant we might find it. Authentic people are honest with themselves. They challenge and question themselves, they look for ways in which they are being self-deceptive and try to see things from different angles. They know what they think, but they are willing to change their views if new information comes their way. As such, authenticity requires openness and the ability to be realistic in how we make sense of what has happened to us.

Authentic people know themselves. They are able to listen to their inner voice – their gut – and they can understand the complexities of their feelings and hear their own inner wisdom. In contrast, people who are alienated from themselves fail to go with their intuitions, they get confused about their emotions and make poor decisions for themselves, instead doing what they think will please others.

Unless we know ourselves well, we can't be trusted to make good decisions in our best interests, nor in anyone else's interests, for that matter. And that applies to the big decisions in life. Think about the jury members who are deciding on the verdict of other people's lives, or the politicians who are making decisions about whether to go to war – such decisions require the clear and clean thinking and behaviour that comes with authenticity.

Sarah, whom we met earlier, knows herself pretty well. Even 20 years ago she was in tune with herself well enough to know her gut feeling was to say no to her boyfriend's marriage proposal. Yet, despite this, she relented. Under pressure, her tendency is to go with what others want from her. She might know herself but what she doesn't do so well, and is only now learning, is to make and then own her decisions.

Own yourself

The authentic person will not let others blind them to their own truth or let others bully them into taking a position that they don't agree with. Solomon Asch was one of the greatest psychologists of the past century. In his autobiography, he recalls from his childhood an event on the evening of his first Passover. He saw his grandmother setting a glass of wine on the table.

> I asked my uncle, who was sitting next to me, why the door was being opened. He replied, 'The prophet Elijah visits this evening every Jewish home and takes a sip of wine from the cup reserved for him.' I was amazed at this news and repeated, 'Does he really come? Does he really take a sip?' My uncle said, 'If you watch very closely, when the door is opened you will see – you watch the cup – you will see that the wine will go down a little.' And that's what happened. My eyes were riveted upon the cup of wine. I was determined to see whether there would be a change. And to me it seemed … that indeed something was happening at the rim of the cup, and the wine did go down a little.[7]

Many years later, as a professor at Harvard University, Asch's memory of this event set the stage for one of the most influential experiments in social psychology. In the wake of the Holocaust, when psychologists were asking how it could be that so many people succumbed to Hitler's will, Asch reflected on the power of social influence. He set out to uncover its effects.

Imagine you have agreed to take part in Asch's experiment. You duly turn up at the expected time. You enter the room and are asked to take your place around a table. There are already five others sitting there. The experimenter explains that you are all taking part in a study of visual perception. He shows you three lines of different lengths and asks you to say whether each of these lines in turn is longer, shorter or the same length as another line that he shows you. Around the table, one by one, everyone gives the same correct answer for the first line. Everything seems straightforward for the second line, too. But for the third line the first person calls out with what seems like the wrong answer. You think the person must have made a mistake. But the second person also gives the same wrong answer – as does the third. You, of course, are looking hard at the lines and wondering what is going on. Then the fourth and fifth people both agree with the others. It is now your turn to give your answer. You look harder at the lines. Are you sure you are right? Do you go with your own eyes?

Unknown to you, this is not an experiment on visual perception. Everyone else in the room is part of a set-up to test whether you will conform to the wisdom of the group. Remarkably, 76 per cent of participants conformed at least once.[8] Like the young Solomon Asch, they gave answers that defied what their eyes were telling them. Perhaps they genuinely began to doubt their own senses or, more likely, they went along with the group simply to fit in. In so many situations in everyday life we are, like Asch's participants, faced with a choice of whether to speak our mind or go along with others. Subsequent studies have confirmed again and again how susceptible many of us are to the power of social influence.

What is often overlooked, however, is that 24 per cent of Asch's participants *did not* conform, even once. Remarkably, this fact is rarely mentioned in the textbooks. Yet Asch himself noted that those who did not conform were confident of their own opinions and did not seem to be concerned with what the majority thought. They held their ground on what they saw.

Authentic people take responsibility for their choices in life. They know that they are the authors of their own lives. They do not shy away from their mistakes by blaming others. But they also do not blame themselves. Taking responsibility is not about blaming yourself by ruminating over how foolish, clumsy, stupid or whatever you think you may have been, but about learning from what has happened and looking to the future with clearer goals and greater wisdom about how to move forward. They know the boundaries of their responsibilities and those of others. They own themselves and they expect others to take their own responsibility.

When we meet people who have a problem, often we rush to try to solve it for them. We offer solutions, encourage them to take a certain action, or whatever, to bring about change. But it is a change that *we* desire: as such we have inadvertently taken responsibility for the other person. It is better to listen to them, allow them to be responsible and do what we can to support them to be the agent of change in their own lives.

Authentic people will not try to control or manipulate others. They respect others' right to be the agents of their own life, because that is what they expect for themselves from others. When faced with attempts to control or manipulate them, authentic people resist external pressures to go along with how others think. They will not conform to ideas, opinions or views because others want them to, or because that is the majority view. They will weigh up evidence for and against an argument, reach their own judgement and hold their ground on what they think rather than compromise themselves.

Authenticity requires us to be able to overcome our desires to fit in and be part of the crowd. The authentic person is not fearless but is willing to feel their fear to be authentic. Think of Henry Fonda in the classic movie *Twelve Angry Men*, which tells

the story of one juror who stands resistant against the other 11
and, over hours locked together with them in a claustrophobic
room, forces them to change their minds. We, as viewers, see
that he was right to stand his ground against the all-too-quick
judgement of guilt made by the others and despite their pressure on him to agree. Most people like to imagine that, if put
in a similarly challenging situation, they too would rise to the
occasion and champion justice, even if other people were against
them. The fact is, of course, that much of the time people don't
rise to the occasion and do the right thing.

In these ways described above, the authentic person owns
their decisions and takes responsibility for their actions, knowing the consequences. They know that no one else is the boss of
them. They are the boss of themselves. By taking responsibility
for themselves and their choices, they are welcoming of feedback from others, curious to see other points of view and always
open to learning about themselves, no matter how painful the
revelations may be.

Be yourself

In 2011, anti-capitalist protesters set up tented communities
in several parts of the Western world. One of these was outside
St Paul's Cathedral in London. At first, the cathedral was clear
in its support for the protestors. But, several days later, when
the protest had become established, the Bishop of London and
the Dean of St Paul's asked the protesters to leave. Why this
change of mind? On the grounds of health and safety, came the
reply. Still the protesters did not leave. The next day the cathedral shut its doors to the public, claiming it wasn't safe to keep
them open. For the first time since the bombing of London in
the Second World War the doors of St Paul's were shut to visitors. But, turning to the public expecting an outcry against the
protesters, the cathedral was surprised to find that it had little

support. The public seemed not to be convinced of the Church of England's story. To the public it looked like the cathedral wanted the protesters to move because their presence had reduced the number of visitors. Income had fallen. The Church of England was seen to have failed to be true to its calling – its spiritual inner nature. The Church was seen as behaving inauthentically. Surely, it should hold to its spiritual purpose and its alignment with the oppressed, not be driven by profit. What is clear is just how highly we value authenticity in others and in our institutions. With authenticity comes integrity.

Think of the people you most admire and those you least admire. The chances are you will find that it is authenticity that differentiates those whom you admire from those you don't. Generally speaking, we admire those who possess self-knowledge, the ability to be honest and transparent and who stand their ground for what they believe in. And we don't admire those we see as fake or phony.

Ironically, people value authenticity so much that often they will do their best to fake it. In a classic study published in 1998, Roos Vonk at Leiden University examined the 'slime effect', which manifests itself when people behave in flattering, supportive and interested ways to those in more powerful positions but ungraciously to those in less powerful positions.[9] We dislike people we see doing this because it betrays a lack of genuineness in their thoughts and actions. To fake authenticity, some people use their knowledge of the slime effect to their own benefit by deliberately behaving in a gracious manner to everyone so there is no flagrant contrast between behaviours towards subordinates and superiors. This makes it more difficult to spot their inauthenticity. Vonk calls it 'mainstream brown-nosing'.

As I've already mentioned, sometimes it can be the wisest choice not to say what we think or feel. However, to live inauthentically day by day as a mainstream brown-noser is not a good life choice. It is better, surely, to work out what you stand for and live your life consistent with your beliefs, values and motivations and be gracious to others simply because it is the right thing to do. Authentic people, and institutions, say what they mean and mean what they say. They are the people we enjoy spending time with and with whom we will share our fears and hopes. They are the institutions we are proud to belong to and whose services we trust. They are the politicians we vote for time and again.

A striking example comes from a study by Jason Teven at California State University.[10] Teven asked people to rate the credibility and deceptiveness of the 2008 US presidential candidates. In a comparison of Hillary Clinton, Barack Obama, John McCain, Rudy Giuliani and John Edwards, Obama came out highest on credibility and lowest on deceptiveness, he was the most liked and – as we all now know – went on to win the election. Of course, we never know the true intentions of someone else, but the notion of authenticity in leadership has attracted new attention after Obama's surprising win.

Given just how much we respect and value those who are willing to be themselves, how come we find it so difficult? Have you ever held back from telling someone how angry you feel with them, or not told someone you cared for that you loved them, not talked openly about your sexual preferences with a partner, or not admitted to a mistake when you ought to? Like Pam, who held back from expressing her feelings to her boss, we think we have good reasons, and in some cases we may have, but much of the time we may be fooling ourselves about our reasons in order to avoid the discomfort of an authentic life. In the longer run, however, we are the losers if we continue to not be ourselves.

The authentic person's inclination is towards openness and transparency with others, but they are not fools. They will refuse to be dragged into needless arguments with people who have no intention of seeing their point of view. They know when the more authentic thing to do is to walk away.

Having examined what it is that authentic people do, I

developed the authenticity formula ҳ
these three things are combined that oɪ.
authentically.

The formula for authentic living

Authentic people know themselves and their motivatic ., they own their decisions and take responsibility in such a way that they will stand up against social pressures and speak the truth as it seems to them, and, in their day-to-day life, they will come across to others as transparent, honest and genuine.

These three things that authentic people do are a powerful trio in all walks of life. Crucially, however, we need to employ all three so that we know ourselves, then the decisions we take ownership of will be the right ones and worth putting into action. In short:

Know yourself + Own yourself + Be yourself =
the Authentic Life

If any one of these three parts is missing, it is not authentic living. You cannot be yourself unless you own yourself and you cannot own yourself unless you know yourself.[11] These three facets of authenticity require us to have a deep courage, humility and the dedication to confront the truth about ourselves, in order to say the difficult things that need to be said and, when pushed, to fight for what we believe to be right.

Such qualities as those described above are vital to success and happiness in all areas of our lives, from parenting to the boardroom and even to the bedroom. The very word 'authentic' is derived from the Greek word *authentikos*, meaning to 'act in one's own authority'. So authenticity is no soft option for life. Living authentically can be terrifying at times, because it means taking responsibility for one's decisions. But the authentic is comfortable with their discomfort.[12] They know what they need to do, and they press on, one step at a time, in full awareness that their actions have consequences.

CASE STUDY: *Andrew*

During the recession of the late 1980s Andrew remembers attending a meeting where his boss, Jason, reassured the group of staff of around 30 people that their jobs were safe. Andrew was Jason's deputy and responsible for the day-to-day running of the organisation. As everyone was leaving the room, Jason called Andrew over. Both of them were wanted at head office. The two men set off in Jason's car and, as they were driving, Jason told Andrew that they needed to lose about 30 per cent of the staff. He said he couldn't say that in the meeting because they needed to maintain morale in the meantime. It was going to be Andrew's job to break the bad news. Andrew's mind was in turmoil. He couldn't believe what he had just heard and how it was the opposite from what Jason had been telling everyone only minutes earlier. 'It went right against how I felt about the way things should be done. I take ethics in business very seriously. I just wasn't going to do this. I was scared witless, but I handed in my resignation. It was probably the best thing I've done.' For Andrew, it was most important that he should act with integrity.

Authenticity is about how we approach life day by day, moment by moment. What that looks like is highly individual for each of us, and what it looks like today might be different from what it looks like tomorrow. Living authentically is hard because there are so many forces influencing us to believe that it is more important to fit in and be liked than to take a risk and speak our truth. Living authentically is an ideal to aspire to, knowing that it is hard and that from time to time we will make mistakes, but always striving to do it better. It is not a state of perfection in which we know exactly what we want from our lives; is it not a position where we can go around needlessly telling people what we think, neither is it being so distinctive that we stand out for the sake of it. It is when we have no need to impress others or gain their attention. We are content to be who we are and for others to see us for who we are. We may not know exactly what our directions in life are right now, but we are doing our best to follow the road that is right for us, rather than the road that others want us to go down. We speak our truths, but we use our wisdom to understand when it is appropriate. If we do stand out, it is for these reasons.

You can change

In keeping with the experiences of Sarah, Pam and Andrew, you too may feel that your life had been derailed in some way and that you are not on the right track. Ask yourself the following questions.

EXERCISE: Are you living a life that is true to yourself?

Do you feel free to make your own choices?
Do you feel free to express your views and opinions?
Do you feel you can be yourself on a day-to-day basis?

If you said no to any of these questions, it might be that you are living a life that is less true to yourself than you would like and that you feel yourself to be off track.

We can change our lives by striving for greater authenticity, but it is an ongoing, life-long journey.

As we embark on that journey, change is inevitable but not necessarily easy. People don't go from an absence of self-understanding to a wealth of self-knowledge from one day to the next. It takes some time to become practised in listening to our inner voice of wisdom. People who are used to putting on an act to impress others will not find it easy to change into the person who is transparent and genuine in their dealings with people. But such change is possible, and with effort, courage and commitment it will happen. As it does, expect a greater sense of freedom, power, happiness and fulfilment to be part of your life.

Before I go any further, let me emphasise that authenticity is not something that people either have or don't have. It is not like a qualification that you get, along with the certificate to hang on the wall. It is about the decisions you make in each and every moment and how you make them.

In essence, authenticity is about realising that we are the authors of our own lives. If we are the authors of our own lives, the secret is not to let someone else hold the pen. It is up to us to choose what we become. I hope in this chapter I have succeeded in showing you that the authentic life is worth pursuing, not only to help you overcome any current difficulties you might be experiencing but also for its own sake, knowing that it is the road to a happier and more fulfilled life. In the following chapters I will go deeper into the question of what authenticity is and the answers from the best minds in psychology.

PART I

How To Be Yourself

What a man can be, he must be. This need we may call self-actualisation.

Abraham Maslow

We are born to be authentic. Authenticity is our natural state. However, balancing the process of realising one's own needs while living together with others, and meeting the needs of those relationships, is not always straightforward. The following chapters explain how we can become derailed and how we can go about regaining our balance.

Chapter 2

We Are Born to Be Ourselves

In my local supermarket recently, I had a flashback to when I was about eight years old. I was in a toy shop. Piled high on the shelves were brightly coloured boxes and inside were model aeroplanes, building blocks, mechanical sets, action figures, puzzles and games. I felt the anticipation of the pleasures they contained. Suddenly, as someone nudged past me with a trolley, I remembered where I was. I looked along the aisle of the supermarket at its pre-packed processed foods in their brightly coloured boxes, with all their promises of novelty and exotic tastes, and I remembered an old psychology experiment by two researchers, James Olds and Peter Milner, in the 1950s.[1] Laboratory rats were wired up so that if they pressed a lever they would get a pleasurable electrical stimulation to their hypothalamus, the part of the brain linked to pleasure. What did the rats do? You guessed it. They spent their time pressing the lever up to 4,000 times an hour. Standing in that supermarket I thought that we in Western society, like Olds and Milner's rats, are constantly striving for hits of pleasure.

Now, before you think that I'm some sort of puritan who believes that pleasure should be banned, let me assure you I'm not. But I do think that we live in a culture in which the pursuit of happiness has become overvalued. The fact is that we can't be happy all of the time. If we expect to be, then we are going to be very disappointed. The endlessly happy life is not possible. Life involves all sorts of experiences, and if we set ourselves the ambition to always be happy, we will fail. Philosophers throughout the ages have understood this.

The sort of happiness we have been talking about up to now is commonly referred to as 'hedonia' – the states associated with pleasure, enjoyment, excitement and comfort. The philosophy of hedonia can be traced back to the Greek philosopher Aristippus of Cyrene. His argument was that pleasure is the highest good to be sought – that we should do all we can to gain pleasure and avoid pain. And of course many people do try to work out what they can do to achieve this, be it through sex, wealth, status and so on.

However, it seems that the more someone focuses their life on hedonism, the less likely they are to find happiness. Rather, their life will be bereft of meaning and lack depth. Instead, it may be characterised by an absence of intimacy with others, objectified sexuality, endlessly seeking satisfaction through the pursuit of materialistic goods and a lack of concern for others and their welfare.

Eudaimonia – seeking to fulfil our potential in life

In recent years, scholars have begun to look at a very different type of happiness: eudaimonia. It was the Greek philosopher Aristotle who proposed the concept of eudaimonia (pronounced u-day-monia) in the 4th century BC in his essay *Nicomachean Ethics*. The term 'eudaimonia' is etymologically based in the Greek words *eu* (good) and *daimon* (spirit) – it is the notion that living in accordance with one's *daimon*, which we take to mean character and virtue, leads to a good life.[2]

Aristotle remains one of the most influential philosophers of all time,[3] writing on a wide range of topics, but for psychologists *Nicomachean Ethics* remains his most influential work. In Aristotle's day, the term 'ethics' did not mean what we think of today as ethics, but rather it was concerned with the question of how to live a good life.

For Aristotle, pleasure-seeking was a vulgar way of life. He understood human beings to be creatures constantly driven towards what is more perfect. In Book I of the *Nicomachean Ethics*, Aristotle clarifies his perfectionism concept: 'Every craft and every line of inquiry and likewise every action and decision, seems to seek some good; that is why some people were right to describe the good as what everything seeks.'[4]

Always striving towards perfection, Aristotle introduces the notion that individuals have potentials yet to be realised. Just as an acorn has within it the potential to be an oak tree – and only an oak tree, not any type of tree, a bird or a daffodil – a fertilised human egg has the potential to be a person, not anything else. Each person has their own unique set of potentials inherent within them. In the Aristotelian view, we are driven to pursue our potential, to be the best versions of ourselves that we can be. For you, that might be to be an artist, a musician, a scholar, a craftsman, an athlete or an explorer. The eudaimonic life is to be had whenever we are in pursuit of fulfilling our potential.

What we need for the eudaimonic life

To realise our potential we need what Aristotle called 'real goods'. By real goods he meant those things that we need for the development of our potential, such as shelter, clothing, food and friends, but also arts, music, literature and culture – those things that will help us *fully realise* our unique potential. In the modern world, there are things that we need to be able to do in the pursuit of fulfilling our potential, and, in this sense, real goods are defined by their necessity to us as individuals.

The obvious example is that we need money, and so it becomes a real good. But there is also what Aristotle referred to as the 'golden mean', which is the right amount of the good: too little and we are in deficit of what we need to pursue our potential, as can be imagined in times of famine where people's potential is literally thwarted; too much and what was a real good becomes an 'apparent good' – something we don't need.

I don't *need* my comic book collection that I have kept from childhood, but I get some pleasure from occasionally browsing through the old issues. Apparent goods are the things we simply don't need. Apparent goods may give us pleasure and joy, but we don't actually need them. We need food but, as my recent trip to the supermarket reminded me, much of the time when we are shopping for food we are seeking apparent goods rather than real goods. Filling our baskets with an overabundance of food, often highly processed in tempting packaging, much of which will be wasted, is a sign that we have crossed the line from shopping for food as real goods to shopping for apparent goods. This is not to say that apparent goods never have any value to us. The important thing is not to confuse them with real goods.

The eudaimonic view is a different way of thinking about happiness to that we are bombarded with in our daily lives by advertisements. These seem to characterise modern life and sell us apparent goods as if they were real goods. The eudaimonic view seems closer to that of our great-grandparents. It is now thought that Thomas Jefferson, who said in the American Declaration of Independence that the pursuit of happiness was an unalienable right, was actually referring to the *eudamionic version* of happiness rather than the *hedonic version*.[5] It makes good sense that the founding fathers of America had the vision that everyone should be given the opportunity to become the best that they could be, rather than their vision being the endless pursuit of pleasure.

Self-actualisation – aiming to be the best version of ourselves

Coming into the 20th century, the humanistic psychologist Abraham Maslow[6] proposed a similar view to Aristotle. Maslow believed that there is a hierarchy of needs, as shown below,[7] that we have as human beings. As our needs are fulfilled, the more we are able to self-actualise the potential within us.[8]

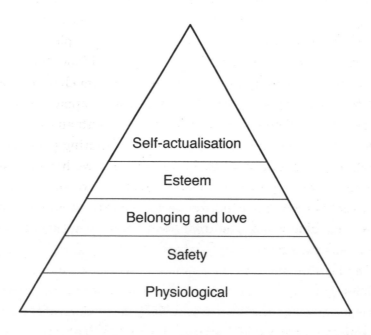

Maslow's hierarchy of needs

At the base of the pyramid there are physiological needs. Physiological needs include things like food, water, sleep and oxygen – very fundamental needs for our survival. A person who is literally starved of these has no other interests but to have these needs satisfied. They will think of little else but their hunger, thirst or illness. Their energy becomes devoted to having these very basic needs met. When these needs are satisfied, they experience a release from tension.

At the next level there are needs for safety. We need relatively stable and secure environments that protect us from the elements and predators, and that will provide us with a predictable environment. Such needs for safety are most often taken for granted by those of us in Western society until we are confronted by real emergencies such as epidemics, riots or disaster. Then we experience fear, anxiety, insecurity, loss and chaos, and our attention turns once again to meeting our needs for safety. When our needs for safety are fulfilled, we experience calm, security and comfort.

Next, are belonging and love needs. We need to be part of a social group because we are social animals. When our needs for love are not satisfied, we are left feeling unwanted, worthless, empty and lonely. When these needs are fulfilled, we feel a sense of warmth, renewed strength within ourselves, and a sense of being whole.

At the next level are esteem needs – our need to value ourselves. Maslow recognised two forms of esteem needs. First, there is a desire for competence and individual achievement. Second, there is a need for appreciation and recognition from others. If these basic needs are not satisfied we feel inferior, incompetent and helpless. When these needs are met, we feel confident, masterful and worthy.

Maslow referred to the above as 'deficit' needs because they describe a state in which the person seeks to obtain something that is lacking. If our deficit needs are not met, we cannot progress to the top of the pyramid. Imagine when your stomach is rumbling with hunger. You can't think of anything but getting something to eat. Or, if you feel empty and lonely, how you will yearn for social contact and a loving relationship. For many people, their lives are consumed by the motivation to satisfy deficiency needs. When needs go unfulfilled for prolonged periods of time, a person may develop distressing and dysfunctional patterns of behaviour.

A deficit need, once satisfied, diminishes in importance, until the need to satisfy it arises again. For those of us fortunate enough to have these deficiency needs met, a higher level of functioning emerges.

The top of the pyramid: using our talents in the best way

When needs at the first four levels are met, our attention turns to being the best version of ourselves that we can be. The top of the pyramid is self-actualisation, which refers to the need people have to be able to use their talents and capacities for what they are best fitted for.

No matter if all our deficiency needs are met, unless we are doing what we are best fitted for, a discontent will arise. As Maslow said, 'people's desire for self-fulfilment, namely, the tendency for them to become actualized in what they are potentially. This tendency might be phrased as the desire to become more and more what one idiosyncratically is, to become everything that one is capable of becoming.'[9]

People differ: there are those who live to seek knowledge and uncover truth; those who are concerned with profit and developing opportunities; those who seek creativity and beauty; those who find meaning in relationships and sharing with others; those driven by power who seek to influence others; and those who seek connection with the spiritual and who quest after deeper understanding beyond the everyday conception of reality.

If we are to be authentic, we need to find a way of living our lives that match our general propensity. In an ideal world, those who seek knowledge and truth might be university lecturers; those concerned with profit and opportunity go into the world of business; those driven by creativity and beauty become designers; those who seek meaning in relationships and sharing with others excel at fundraising and activism; those who are driven by power and the need to influence seek positions in government; and those with a spiritual quest find a life in the church.

In essence, as Maslow said, 'a musician must make music, an artist must paint and a poet must write, if he is to be ultimately at peace with himself'. Of course, although we, or those we know, might seem to fit clearly into one category or the other, for most people there is probably some overlap. It might be, for example, that there are two categories that you cannot choose between when thinking about yourself.

There are also people who, in less obvious ways, have found a match by developing new niches in traditional careers or opening new avenues, such as the person driven by power who enters university life but who climbs the administration ladder to become a leader in that setting; or the truth seeker who goes into politics but ends up behind the scenes developing policy; or the person seeking profit and opportunities who goes into the world of art and ends up developing a design business.

The realisation of our potential to self-actualisation is thwarted when we do not get our needs fully satisfied. Think about Maslow's hierarchy in relation to your current life. Which level of it currently dominates your life? Perhaps you are mostly concerned with self-esteem and finding a way to feel valued about yourself, or perhaps it is about belonging that currently preoccupies you. As you think about this, you might notice that over the course of your life the level that dominates has changed. The levels that dominated a few years ago might be different from those right now. It is not that as we reach one level it is a permanent state, but rather we can move up and down the hierarchy.

To flourish, we need to move up the hierarchy so that we

become engaged in trying to grow as close as possible to the blueprint inside us that holds the secret to our potentialities. For Maslow, if we are less than we are capable of being, then we will be unhappy. Our task is to get to know ourselves and to begin to develop our strengths, express our talents and use our abilities. In this way we become more than we currently are. Each of us is born with our own unique propensities of personality, mental ability and talent, whether that of the athlete, artist, parent, teacher or whatever.

The characteristics of self-actualised people

We can see that Maslow's self-actualisation is another way of expressing the Aristotelian view of the eudaimonic life. According to Maslow, self-actualised people share several characteristics. These people are:

- Efficient in how they perceive reality
- Accepting of themselves, of other people and nature
- Tolerant of uncertainty
- Spontaneous in their thoughts and emotions
- Able to form deep relationships with other people
- Appreciative and grateful in their approach to life
- Thoughtful with a non-hostile sense of humour
- Continually deriving inspiration and strength from life
- Well adjusted to culture but not immersed in it unthinkingly
- Sufficiently guided by their own inner goals and values
- Not ashamed or frightened of their emotions
- Able to express their emotions freely and clearly
- Understanding that it is better to be yourself than to be popular
- Not seeking of other people's approval
- Aware of their own weaknesses and strengths[10]

Maslow's work is widely known, but it is often misunderstood in three ways.

First, according to Maslow, self-actualisation is a state that continues to grow, so it is not the case that we reach an ideal and stop but that we are continually seeking further challenges, learning and opportunities to develop our understandings of ourselves and the world around us. Specifically, those who are self-actualised continue to be motivated by intrinsic values such as 'truth, goodness, beauty, perfection, excellence, simplicity, elegance, and so on', values that go beyond their self-interest.[11]

Second, Maslow was not painting a naive picture of self-actualised people who had reached a state of perfection. Self-actualised people may feel somewhat detached from the world around them and perhaps even be seen by others as ruthless, so dedicated can they be to the pursuit of what matters to them. In his interviews with people he considered to have attained a high level of self-actualisation, Maslow did not claim these people were perfect. While such people had achieved some level of greatness they were also very human. As Maslow wrote:

> There do in fact exist creators, seers, sages, saints, shakers and movers. This can certainly give us hope for the future of the species even if they are uncommon and so not come by the dozen. And yet these very same people can at times be boring, irritating, petulant, selfish, angry, or depressed.[12]

Even if we succeed in achieving a level of self-actualisation, we still encounter the difficulties and challenges of life, but we face them with greater psychological maturity.

Third, the most important point of Maslow's theory that is often overlooked is that self-actualisation was the default state for human beings. Maslow said, 'I think of the self-actualizing man not as an ordinary man with something added, but rather as the ordinary man with nothing taken away.'[13] The natural inbuilt tendency towards self-actualisation can be likened to the force of gravity and how water will always run downhill.[14] If we pour a glass of water it will quickly find its way to the lowest point. It's inevitable. But in the same way that the flow of water can be halted by blocking its natural course, the actualisation of our potential can be thwarted if the environment does not support our basic psychological needs. It is for this reason that not everyone attains a high level of self-actualisation.

What is human nature?

As we saw, the Aristotelian view is that the fulfilled life arises from performing activities that reflect one's true calling. To put it another way, it is the idea that well-being consists in nature-fulfilment.

Aristotle's view of human nature is an intriguing one that pushes us to ask ourselves what the nature of human beings actually is. What does it mean to become a person? What are the deep-seated defining features of people? Imagine you are visited by Martians, who have just visited the planet Earth. They are explorers to this planet and they ask you, 'What are human beings like?' What would you say? What three words would you use to best describe humans? Did you use negative words like greedy, violent and selfish or did you use positive words like creative, collaborative and caring?

How we understand human nature is not an idle question but the most important one that we will confront in this book. If authenticity is about realising one's potential, then, we have to ask, what is the potential within the human species that we should want to encourage? Each person will have their own unique potentials, but what I'm referring to are the universal potentials that characterise all people. We know that acorns are destined to be oak trees. We know the nature of oak trees: they grow tall, sturdy and reach out with their branches and foliage in the fullest way they can. Imagine an acorn that has fulfilled its potential as an oak tree to its fullest. What does it look like? Then ask yourself, what characterises human beings who most fulfil their potential as human beings?

For the humanistic psychologists such as Maslow, self-actualisation is the natural state of human beings. When we are at our most authentic, these are the ways in which we will be, because it is the nature of human beings to be that way. Seen this way, authenticity is to be valued, encouraged and nurtured in each and every one of us.

Of course, if you don't see it that way, then the whole notion of authenticity is to be challenged. And you wouldn't be on your own. Sigmund Freud, the father of psychoanalysis, also had a very pessimistic view of human nature. For Freud, humans were lustful murderous savages if they followed their natural instincts, and it was only through civilisation that we learned to keep checks and balances on our destructive nature. To a Freudian, therefore, it would seem ridiculous to advocate authenticity.

The lasting effects of a Freudian view

When Maslow and the other humanistic psychologists started writing in the 1950s and 1960s, their ideas were seen as controversial, because Freudian views were still popular at that time. Indeed, they still are. Freud's view is the ghost in the machine that continues to haunt us to this day. The notion that we are murderous savages at heart permeates Western culture in all its aspects, from parenting to education to public policies that serve to restrict and control people. Because of this deeply entrenched idea, many of our institutions are founded on the notion that people need to be tightly regulated, monitored and shaped into being healthy and constructive members of society.

Maslow and the other humanistic psychologists challenged

Freudian thinking about human nature, and its implications for how we organise our institutions. Their view was that we don't need institutions to restrict and control us in order to shape us into constructive members of society; rather we need institutions that meet our basic needs. Only then will we be able to fulfil our potential in ways that are most constructive and rewarding to ourselves and those around us.

One other influential scholar who took a similar view was Karen Horney.[15] According to Horney, we cannot be taught to be ourselves, but when we are raised in a favourable environment in which we are given the opportunity to grow we are free to become ourselves. She wrote:

> ... whether for ourselves or for others, the ideal is the liberation and cultivation of the forces which lead to self-realization.[16]

As a psychologist, I believe that the above debate over the nature of being human is important. After all, it is a fundamental question whether our aim is to control or liberate people's essential nature. Modern-day positive psychologists, who we will meet later, are also coming round to the latter view, adopting Aristotelian principles, looking back to the work of Maslow and generating new and exciting research that supports the view that if our basic needs as human beings are satisfied then we will tend to move in self-actualising and ultimately authentic ways.

Maslow's hierarchy is a powerful way to understand what authenticity is – it is the behaviours, thoughts and feelings of a person whose basic needs have been met. But, as already mentioned, not everyone has their needs met, in which case their strivings towards authenticity are blocked.

Indeed, we might be born to be authentic, but we are also all too easily derailed from our inbuilt destiny to be our best. In the next chapter I will look more closely at how we become derailed.

Chapter 3

How We Become Derailed From Being Ourselves

Next to Abraham Maslow, one of the most renowned humanistic psychologists of the 20th century was Carl Rogers. Like Maslow, Rogers thought that it was the normal and natural urge of human beings to be motivated towards fulfilment, towards actualisation and being all that they can be.[17] Rogers also recognised that this natural urge could be thwarted when a person's needs go unsatisfied. Famously, Rogers told a story from his childhood about a potato bin in the basement of the family farm where he grew up. It was here that the family stored their winter supply of potatoes. The bin was several feet below a small window. He noticed how, unlike the healthy green shoots that potatoes sprout when planted in the soil, the potatoes stored in the basement produced pale, white and unhealthy looking sprouts:

> ... these sad, spindly sprouts would grow 2 or 3 feet in length as they reached toward the distant light of the window. The sprouts were, in their bizarre, futile growth, a sort of desperate expression of the directional tendency ... They would never become plants, never mature, never fulfil their real potential.[18]

Rogers wrote of how he thought of these potatoes when he encountered people in the back wards of state hospitals in his job as a psychologist.[19] Like Rogers's potato plants, those whose lives are warped through restrictive environments that fail to meet their basic psychological needs, will in their own ways end up twisted, dysfunctional and bizarre.[20] And, as with Rogers's potato plants – their sprouts striving towards the distant light in their best effort to achieve their potential – such people are also striving to be the best that they can under their circumstances.

Humanistic psychologists like Rogers are often mistakenly thought of as being somewhat 'Pollyannaish' with their talk of people actualising their potential, but as the above analogy makes clear, describing how a plant needs sunlight to thrive does not imply that we will have endless sunshine. Rather, like Rogers, we think about what happens when the sun doesn't shine.[21]

CASE STUDY: *Michael*

Michael grew up with a violent father and so he learned very quickly to be sensitive to his father's shifts in mood. His father could very quickly explode with anger at the slightest provocation, more often imagined than real. Not surprisingly, Michael became skilled at sensing the emotional temperature of others and quickly placating them with humour. This served him well in the presence of his violent father. Thirty years later Michael is an upbeat and friendly man whom others would describe as laid back. Far from it: inside, Michael lives on the edge, always alert to how others are reacting. Even though his father is now dead and there is no longer any real danger of violence, he lives in a high state of alert, as if at any moment those around him will explode with anger and criticism. His joking around and easy-going demeanour is a mask designed to placate others.

People develop whatever patterns of behaviour, and ways of relating to the world, it takes to help them survive in their immediate adverse circumstances. However, as with Michael, such patterns of behaviour become habitual and get carried forward into adulthood, irrespective of whether or not they remain useful to us. They have become maladaptive. None of Michael's colleagues knew that he was on psychiatric medication, and few would even have suspected that he had a problem with anxiety.

CASE STUDY: *Joanne*

Joanne had a similarly difficult childhood, but she learned to fight back. Always the target of criticism from her mother, she quickly learned that the best form of defence was attack. Twenty years on, with a reputation for being a punitive manager and prone to sarcastic outbursts, colleagues give Joanne a wide berth at work, knowing that she is difficult to deal with. They know that she is likely to misinterpret what they say as criticism, even when it is not intended, so they tread carefully.

Michael and Joanne would say that this is just who they are. They see the world as they do and don't think of themselves as unusual. But what Rogers was saying was that these selves are masks, built over many years. For some, these patterns become so entrenched and dysfunctional that they may have mental health difficulties.[22]

As Joanne's colleagues have learned, people exhibiting such distorted personalities are difficult to deal with. Such people have a view of themselves and of the situation that is distorted and unrealistic, but the main problem is their rigidity. They are not open to challenge and change. Alternative points of view feel like a threat to the person's very existence.

The person themselves, however, would not describe what they do in this way. Joanne sees herself as someone with a good sense of humour, who does not take fools lightly and doesn't beat around the bush when something needs to be said. She is unaware of just how punitive and defensive she comes across. Her picture of herself is at odds with how others see her. Joanne would not recognise that she has problems of a psychological nature.

Michael does recognise that he has problems. He has spoken about his anxiety to his GP, who prescribed medication to help him cope. The medication seems to help to get him through the day, but Michael doesn't understand why he feels as he does. In fact, he has never actually given it much thought. He hasn't connected the way he feels to how it was for him growing up in a violent household. The medication doesn't help him make sense of the fact that he has such feelings of anxiety because of the psychological tension he still carries around from his childhood.

In short, we learn as children, through watching our parents or other caregivers, what to expect and how to behave. Those whose lives are warped through chaotic, controlling or rejecting environments are derailed in their authentic development. Some may not recognise that they have psychological difficulties; others may recognise the fact but fail to grasp how these problems have arisen.

On the other hand, those who experience ordered, nurturing and accepting environments that succeed in meeting their basic psychological needs go on to flourish, like the healthy green shoots of potato plants grown outside. Rogers believed that as biological creatures we are constantly striving to become the best and most authentic versions of ourselves that we can be. Put another way, like the acorn knows in what directions it has to grow to realise its potential, so too do human beings.[23]

The newborn infant is authentic

Imagine for a second that you are looking into the cot of a newborn infant. We don't need to teach the newborn infant to be authentic. It already is. As infants, we are in tune with what is going on inside us. We have no façade in our outer expression. As we watch the infant in her cot, it is clear that she is a bundle of authentic experiences of her feelings. When she cries, gurgles or smiles, these are genuine expressions of an inner state. There is no façade or pretence to be other than she is in that moment. If the infant is too warm, cold, hungry or in pain, she will respond in a way that is true to the experience of these sensations.

Of course, at this stage of life she has not yet developed self-awareness. All experiences she has are just what they are. Pain, hunger or discomfort are all experienced just as they are and without evaluation. When hungry, she cries. When fed, she feels full. When no longer hungry, she stops crying. As human beings at this stage of life, we are a ceaseless flow of feelings. The psychologist William James said, 'The baby, assailed by eyes, ears, nose, skin, and entrails at once, feels it all as one great blooming, buzzing confusion.'[24] As infants, feelings arise within us in relation to changes in our external world or from within us. We don't have words for what is going on, but our face, body and movements express authentically those feelings bubbling up from within us. The infant is not yet able to sort experiences into different categories. This comes later.

As infants, we begin to crawl and to reach out as we explore the world around us. Attracted by certain sounds, colours, tastes, noises and sensations, we move towards those. All of these are not conscious decisions but the inherent tendency towards realisation of our potentialities. In Rogers's view, we are born with an innate drive to be the best version of ourselves that we can be. As infants, we explore the world around us in relation to how well it satisfies our needs for realisation of our psychological potential. The infant reaches out and touches colourful objects that it is attracted to. The infant does not make conscious decisions, but moves just like Rogers's potato plant does towards sunlight, always striving to become the potentialities contained within.

Infants, however, are vulnerable and their authenticity is an extremely fragile process that is all too easily derailed in the following years as self-awareness begins to develop. On average, the capacity for self-awareness develops around 18 months of age. We know this from some ingenious studies of infants looking at themselves in mirrors. Have you ever seen a dog looking in a mirror? If you have you will know that the dog doesn't seem to recognise itself. What it does is snarl at its image as if it's another animal encroaching on its territory. This is how most non-humans respond.[25] Infants, on the other hand, recognise themselves.

In a ground-breaking study, 96 infants had a blob of paint put on their noses. Each was observed looking in a mirror before and after the paint was applied. Infants younger than 12 months did not seem to recognise themselves, but from around 15 months they began to touch themselves on the nose when they looked in the mirror. By 24 months most were touching their noses[26] – a sure sign that they recognised themselves and had developed self-awareness.

Human beings are storytellers

With self-awareness comes the need to construct a positive narrative about who we are – the sense of self – all the feelings, attitudes, desires, judgements and behaviours that eventually we consider ours and which we take to define ourselves. As children, we are spontaneous and creative. We will experiment with things, trying out new activities and figuring out how things work, and without hindrance we will do this in such a way that we learn about ourselves, the world and how we best fit within the world. The infant is learning to sort experiences into different categories and to make a difference between 'me' and 'not me' experiences.

The sense of self develops as the child interacts with the people around him, the picture of self becoming more complex as the child has more and more experiences, each building on the last. Children learn to tell a story about who they are. This story is the map for how to live their life.

Our childhood picture can become distorted

'I said I'd like to be a writer when I'm older and my father looked at me and said, "Well you won't have much chance of that."' As Chris told me this story from her childhood, her voice trembled. Even now, all these years later, this moment in her life still haunts her. Her dreams were dashed to the ground. 'I learned that I wasn't any good and I should not say anything.'

What happens is that through our interactions with others we develop our sense of self. Particularly important are those interactions that are evaluative in some way. Through these more evaluative interactions, our picture of ourselves may become distorted. Comments that are not intended as evaluative can nonetheless stick in children's minds.

Lydia moved to a new school when she was 13. She was introduced to the class by her new teacher who said, 'We already have a Lydia in the class. We call her lovely Lydia. We will just have to call you Lydia.' Lydia told me this story many years after it happened, because even now in her late twenties she remembers how in that moment she defined herself as 'not lovely'.

David was the youngest of four children. He recalls how his mother used to call him the 'perfect son'. Now in his early thirties, always well tailored and expensively groomed, he does all he can to appear perfect, even to strangers. He expects perfection in himself and looks for the same in others. Not surprisingly, David is lonely, and although he has had many romantic encounters he can't find a long-term partner as each and every woman he meets he finds less than perfect, whether it be a slightly crooked nose, a scar or a birthmark.

We also learn how we should be in the world. Anthony remembers being violently reprimanded by his father when he was about 13 for something he had done wrong. The only thing was he hadn't done anything wrong. Anthony recalled how that day, sitting by himself on the school bus, he thought to himself, 'If I am going to be beaten for being bad, I might as well be bad.' That was the day Anthony took up smoking because, to him, it was what bad boys did. Almost 40 years later he has tried to stop smoking many times but still struggles with his habit.

As young people, we interpret what is said to us in ways that are often unintended. Peter was only eight when at a school prize day his classmate, Robert, was awarded a prize. At the front of the room before she handed out the prize the teacher said how Robert had worked hard during the year and was a good boy who was always friendly. Peter remembers thinking to himself that he worked hard, was good and always friendly, 'I'm all of those things too.' Peter says that in that moment he learned that the world was unfair. It was clear to him that Robert didn't deserve the prize any more than him or many of the other children in the class.

It is, therefore, that over time we begin to interpret our experiences and make meaning of them. From the shoes we choose to wear to how we have our hair groomed, we are telling a story about who we are. Human beings are storytellers constantly creating a picture of themselves. Along the way the picture becomes a mask.

Unconditional love keeps us on track

Rogers described one of the most important ideas in psychology of all time: unconditional positive regard. So widely known is this idea that it has become hugely misunderstood. Offering someone unconditional positive regard is not about being nice to them, it is about doing what you can to satisfy their basic psychological needs.

Like Maslow, whom we met in the previous chapter, Rogers understood that people had basic psychological needs. Accepting that there are basic needs for survival, and so on, Rogers's attention was focused on two basic human psychological needs.

First, we have the need to be the agent of our own destiny, free to choose our own path without feeling controlled. Children are born with a basic need for agency that drives their exploration of the world.

Second, we need to have a sense of belonging. We are social creatures with a basic need for connection and attachment – especially infants, who are completely dependent on the adults around them.

In Rogers's view, we need to have relationships that are unconditional. By unconditional, he meant relationships that support the young child's freedom to have agency over their own lives and to find their own directions in life. At the same time, those relationships need to nurture the child's need for belonging, in a manner that allows them to feel positively regarded.

To have both needs for agency and belonging met in our relationships provides us with the magic mix that allows us to flourish. The perfect caregiving relationships for children are characterised by unconditional positive regard where the children are loved for who they are, no matter what they do. Surrounded by unconditional positive regard, they are free to be themselves, to be the agents of their own explorations into the world and yet they will know that they are accepted and valued.[27] With their basic psychological needs met, children will flourish and develop in such a way as to realise their unique potentials. The authentic parent finds the right balance such that their child's needs for belonging and agency are equally met. Authentic parents offer their children the freedom to be themselves and to remain loved for being themselves.

Love, regardless of your child's choice of direction

When I visited John and Veronica for the first time, having not met them before, I was surprised to see their young son, Adam, come running down the stairs dressed as a princess and waving a magic wand. Adam ran past us into the kitchen. I was taken by surprise.

Now, I don't have any concern if boys want to dress differently than convention dictates, but it is still fairly unusual to see, and it being my first visit to their home I was surprised. But my surprise quickly gave way to admiration as I saw how both of his parents looked on without any sign of judgement on Adam's choice to dress as a princess. They were as comfortable as if he had appeared dressed as a cowboy or an astronaut.

Unconditional positive regard really means loving your children no matter what directions they choose and giving them the freedom to make their own choices. This is not to say that children should be permitted to do absolutely anything they like without supervision or without providing information about the likely consequences of their actions, but good parenting is a moment-by-moment interaction with our children in such a way that we are constantly trying to get the balance right between supporting their developing agency in the world and simultaneously letting them know that they are valued and accepted for who they are.

Conditional regard throws us off track

Frank was born 30 years earlier than Adam above. When Frank was about 11 years old he told me that he remembers putting on his older sister's clothing one day and was in his bedroom wearing her high-heeled boots when his father walked in. Frank remembers that his father shouted and slapped Frank across the face. It was never mentioned again and Frank never dared to do it again, until many years later when he had left home. As a boy, Frank learned that he should always act like a man if he was to be valued.

From the outset, many parents will actively encourage their children to adopt the gender role that they desire for the child, and won't necessarily see their actions as being an infringe-ment of the child's agency. If your real desire is that your child dresses like a cowboy and not a princess, or a princess and not a cowboy, you can bet that your child will pick up your desires for them. And insofar as they desire your love, they may seek to be the person you want them to be rather than be true to themselves.

Encouraging our children to adopt gender roles, be it a cowboy or a princess, is one example of how we place expectations on our children that may restrict and derail them from being themselves. Think about the weight of all the aspirations, expectations and hopes that we have for our children and what that can do to them. Sam is in her forties. She never leaves her home unless she has put on her make-up to perfection. She describes how she was singled out in her family as the beautiful one. That gave her a special place in her father's affection, and meant she avoided the scoldings her siblings would often receive. She learned that being beautiful meant you were loved and that belief has stuck and influenced her pattern of behaviour to this day.

In reality, we are often surrounded not by unconditional love but by *conditional* love. Sam, who was told constantly by her parents how proud they were of how pretty she was, learns that to be loved and valued she must be attractive. The boy, whose coach shouts at him for missing the kick, learns that to be valued he must be athletic. The child, whose school report is poor and whose parents react with anger, soon learns that to be loved and valued one must do well at school.

To some extent or other we all pick up the rules for how to be, whether we learn that we must be attractive, popular, sporty, tidy, respectful, funny – whatever it is we learn that we must do to belong or be loved.

It is in this way that children begin doing whatever it takes to please others. Our need to belong is so strong that, while we are children, it suppresses our need for agency. In short, we work so hard at doing what it takes to please others that we fail to learn about ourselves and our own directions in life.

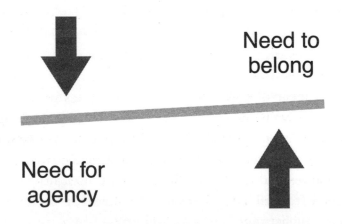

The need to belong suppresses the need for agency
in a conditional relationship

Chaotic, controlling and rejecting environments that fail to meet the basic psychological needs described by Rogers lead the child to be constricted by fear, to feel unsafe and anxious, and unable to explore the world around them. Thus the stage is set for a life of self-alienation. For some, like Frank, the conditional regard is overwhelming and reinforced by violence, such that the child's natural instinct towards authenticity is thwarted. For others, the conditional influences are more subtle but are still damaging to the child's ability to be authentic and develop their potential.[28]

The effects of controlling behaviour

The perfect parent is unconditionally accepting all the time, but of course the perfect parent doesn't exist. We all make mistakes, have blind spots, and even if we were actually perfect some of the time our intentions may still be misunderstood. Our best-intentioned behaviour can be misread by children. In Rogers's view, to some extent or other everyone carries some baggage from their childhood and, as such, few people ever realise their full potential. Most people realise only a portion at best of their full potential. For others the realisation of their potential is severely thwarted.

It's not easy to strike the balance all the time. Good parenting does not mean always getting it right. What it means is always *striving* to get it right. In the ideal world all we would have is unconditional love as children, and in that way we would have the safety of the sense of belonging that allows us to flourish, to be ourselves and to develop our potential. Conditional regard can come from all the authority figures in children's lives: parent figures, teachers and religious educators, media and television. It makes sense to offer conditional relationships to children if you think that they need to be moulded into the right shape, but not if you go along with Rogers in his belief about human nature that the natural state of authenticity is itself the most desired one.

Rogers summarised how his work to liberate people was in tune with the ancient Chinese philosophy of Lao-tzu.[29] The book attributed to Lao-tzu is the *Tao Te Ching* (pronounced Dow Deh Jing), which translates as 'The Book of the Way'.[30] The core of the philosophy is *wei wu wei*, which translates as 'doing not-doing'.

- If I keep from meddling with people, they take care of themselves,
- If I keep from commanding people, they behave themselves,
- If I keep from preaching at people, they improve themselves,
- If I keep from imposing on people, they become themselves.[31]

This ancient Chinese philosophy, Rogers thought, expressed similar views to his own about the power of unconditional positive regard in creating relationships that allowed people to be at their best.

Since Rogers, other researchers have developed these ideas further and the evidence is good that Rogers was on the money with his theory of child development and how controlling figures in a child's life can have a detrimental effect. In one study, 26 children aged 6 or 7 years were observed playing. In the room were children's magazines, jigsaw puzzles, building blocks and so on. But what the researchers, Richard Ryan and Edward Deci at the University of Rochester, were really interested in was how mothers interacted with the children. Watching from behind a one-way screen, the researchers categorised controlling statements made by the mother into those that pressure the child to do something, distract the child's attention from what they are doing, imply conditional worth, use words such as 'should' and so on (for example, 'Good, that's just what you should do', 'Don't you think you should use smaller building blocks for that?' or 'You are a good boy for doing that'). The children had been watched beforehand when they were on their own to establish what they freely liked doing and what interested them the most. When mothers were controlling, children spent less time on the things they freely liked doing – the things that they were intrinsically motivated to do.

Decades of research such as that of Ryan and Deci and their colleagues, confirm the basic ideas that for children to flourish their basic psychological needs must be met and that contexts in which rewards are used to control behaviour undermine the development of intrinsic goals and values.[32] Their research studies show that if we attempt to change people through the use of threats, deadlines, demands, external evaluation and imposed goals, intrinsic motivation is diminished. What is important for the development of authenticity is the provision of opportunities for self-direction, as it provides the person with a greater sense of autonomy.

Teachers and parents who support autonomy in their students foster a higher level of authenticity in their students, leading to more intrinsic motivation and ultimately better performance. Controlling parental and teaching styles lead to a loss of initiative in children and, in the end, despite the intentions of parents and teachers, less effective learning.

In another study by Glen Nix and his colleagues, college students were asked to imagine themselves either taking a class that they wanted to attend but which was not part of their course requirement or a course they did not want to attend but that was a part of their course requirement. Then they were asked to imagine receiving a high grade. Those who imagined taking the class voluntarily reported feeling more vital and alive.[33]

As parents, we need to be less controlling and conditional and more authentic in ourselves, which allows our children the freedom to grow into being more of themselves and to feel more alive and vital, and it also gives them us as a role model for authentic living.[34]

Finding the self-knowledge to move forward

Finally, understanding how our childhood experiences shape our levels of authenticity is important, not because it leads us to endlessly blame our parents, teachers and other caregivers and spend our time looking back at what went wrong, but rather it provides us with the self-knowledge to move forward in life. As adults, our choice is to ruminate on the past or to learn from our experience and think clearly about our futures. The point of rummaging around in our childhoods is not to get lost there but to understand where it is that the voices of others, to go back to Steve Jobs's quote in Chapter 1, originally came from. This is the focus of the next chapter.

Chapter 4

Learn to Listen to Your Own Inner Voice of Wisdom

I remember some 20 years ago walking through Regent's Park in London on a bright sunny day. There was a sign saying not to walk on the grass, and out of the corner of my eye I saw a young boy, perhaps around seven years old, running along the grass, singing and laughing. I turned when I heard what I assume was his father's voice shouting in a scolding voice to get off the grass. I watched the boy glance over at me, then hang his head in humiliation and run back to his parent. The event took only seconds and perhaps was instantly forgotten by the father, and maybe the boy himself has no memory of it 20 years later, but you can be sure that in that young boy's brain new rules for living were being imprinted.

The effects of unconditional love

Avi Assor and colleagues at Ben Gurion University examined how parents interact with their children.[35] One hundred and ten

university students completed a questionnaire asking them to
rate how much they agreed with statements about their parents,
for example:

- As a child, my parents only showed me affection when I
  did well at school.
- As a child, my parents were more loving towards me when
  I was well-behaved.
- As a child, my parents only showed me affection when I
  did well at sports.[36]

Each statement reflects a different desire of the parent: the
first, for the child to do well at school; the second, for them to
be well-behaved; and the third, for them to do well at sports.
In this way the researchers were able to gauge how much social
pressure the students felt their parents had put on them by being
conditional with their affection.

Parents can be conditional with their affection in two ways:
by withholding their love when their child does not behave as
they wish, or by showing their love only when their child does
what they want.

What the researchers found was that those who agreed with
such statements as those above were more likely to be living lives
in which their life goals were things they felt that they *should*
do rather than what they *wanted* to do, they experienced guilt
and shame when they failed to live up to the demands and they
experienced only fleeting satisfaction when they did achieve
success. And they resented their parents.[37]

Intriguingly, the researchers also asked the parents themselves to rate the questions in relation to their own parents,
finding that those parents whose own upbringings were characterised by their parents withholding affection were those
most likely to pass this on to their own children. Ironically, it
seems, the damaging habits of parents may be passed down the

generations. But as we become more authentic ourselves we can reverse this.

Sarah, whom we met earlier, realised that she had developed a need to please her parents through being successful, but she also began to understand that she was repeating the same message to her daughter, Andrea. She was horrified to realise that she was doing this. Sarah began to listen more attentively to Andrea and to be more cautious in how she spoke to her. She wanted her to know that although she hoped she would do well at school she was loved no matter how well she did, just for being her.

Helping our children to develop self-worth

As parents, we need to set limits for our children that have a meaningful rationale. But at the same time we need to learn how not to use controlling language and the withdrawal of affection to get what we want from our children. If we want to help our children find their own authentic directions in life, it involves us making genuine attempts to take our children's perspective. This does not mean overindulgence. Overindulgent parents who promote inflated images of their children's abilities can lay the groundwork for false self-esteem. Their children become unrealistic about themselves and their abilities. High self-esteem, when not grounded in the reality of accomplishments in life, can be the harbinger for aggressive behaviour and narcissism. Rather, we should be concerned that children learn to develop self-worth that is both realistic and based on values and aspirations important to them, rather than a pseudo self-esteem.

Christopher Mruk, at Bowling Green State University in Ohio, describes how authentic self-esteem consists of a high level of self-worth coupled with a high level of actual competence. Authentic self-esteem is healthy for people because it provides them with the inner resources not to be afraid of life but to explore new opportunities and face new challenges. This is essential for us to be able to do if we are to flourish to our full potential. Not only that, but authentic self-esteem also gives us the power to pick ourselves up again when we fail and to move forward having learned from our experiences.[38]

For sure, children will sometimes do things that go against what their parents desire for them, but the challenge is to continue relating to our children without withdrawing affection and implying that the children are unlovable for not doing as we wish. Of course, we might feel disappointment, but the important message to convey is that we are disappointed with the children's actions, not with them as people.

When children do behave in ways that disappoint us, however, we have to question our own expectations. Sometimes we will realise that we have set expectations that are not right for our children. But at other times it is a signal that our children do not comprehend the value of what we are trying to teach them. If so, the solution is still to take a genuine interest in the child's perspective and to help them understand the value of schoolwork, sports, or whatever the issue might be, but always maintaining affection for them as a person, letting them develop their agency in life and to find their own best directions.

It can be tempting for parents to withhold affection in order to shape their children, but it does have damaging psychological consequences, ones that therapists encounter every day in their clinics as people talk about feeling lost in their lives, confused over their directions and lacking a sense of meaning and purpose. It may take many psychotherapy sessions, but as the inner world of the patient is unravelled, all too often such feelings are found to be the core cause of the patient's depression and anxiety.

Steve Jobs, as I mentioned earlier, warned us not to let the noise of others' opinions drown out our own inner voice. We carry all the voices from the past within us about what is expected of us and how we should behave. It is this chatter that creates the roadblock to authenticity and which drowns out our own inner voices of wisdom. Often, we don't even recognise this inner chatter as belonging to others because it has become so much a part of the picture we hold of ourselves. If we are to learn about ourselves, we have to untangle our inner voice of wisdom from these other voices and, in so doing, learn how these other voices have influenced us.

Conditional love creates conditions of worth

Carl Rogers referred to these other voices as our 'conditions of worth': the rules we learn in childhood when the love we get is conditional. Everybody has their own unique combination of conditions of worth. For one person it might be to please other people. For someone else it is to be the smart one. For others it is to always keep their feelings in check.

Conditions of worth become the base for the unforgiving voices in our head that constantly criticise us. Look how fat you are. Look how stupid you are. Look how useless you are. To live an authentic life our task is to not let these voices drown out our own inner voices of wisdom but to learn to listen deeply to ourselves and to know what is going on within us through our intuitions, hunches and feelings at each moment.

Maslow described how he would encourage his students to learn for themselves to listen to their own voices. To illustrate what he meant, he gave the example of when we are given a glass of wine and asked if we like it: often we will look at the label first to see if that gives us any clues as to whether we *ought* to like it. Instead of doing this, he suggested:

I recommend that they close their eyes if possible and that they 'make a hush.' Now they are ready to look within themselves and try to shut out the noise of the world so that they may savor the wine on their tongues and look to the 'Supreme court' inside themselves.[39]

It is all too easy in the rush of everyday life not to give ourselves the time, solitude and stillness to pay attention to what is genuinely going on inside ourselves; to make sense of the confusion of thoughts, feelings and sensations, and, to use Maslow's phrase, look to the supreme court inside us.

Of course, it is not just with a glass of wine that we need to listen to our own inner voices, but with all the decisions we face on a daily basis. The root of many people's problems in living is that they are not in touch with what's important to them and they are confused about their feelings and not able to deal with experiences that threaten their picture of themselves. They may avoid situations in which they will be confronted by the truth about themselves and prefer to put up with doing things that keep them in their comfort zone. They may avoid new opportunities. Unrealistic self-critical inner dialogue in which we tell ourselves we are not good enough or we put ourselves down, or we feel like failures or blame ourselves for misfortunes, all result in leaving us defeated and prone to mental-health problems.[40]

Even positive things that do not fit our picture of ourselves we have to push away. Have you ever been offered a compliment and your first reaction is to be embarrassed, change the topic of conversation, or laugh it off? If so, it might be that your reaction tells you something about your conditions of worth. People who think poorly of themselves will often deny the validity of any compliments that they receive.[41] They are protecting the negative self-image of themselves by pushing away compliments. Next time you find yourself pushing away a genuine compliment, stop. Instead, look the other person in the eye and thank them.

If we are to become more authentic we need to know ourselves better. We need to combat our conditions of worth. Joanne's condition of worth is always to be right. Not surprisingly, she spends a portion of her time arguing with family members and friends, trying to persuade them to see things differently and change their minds. As a result, she is often angry and resentful. The times she can be the least herself are when she is at work and decisions need to be made, triggering her need to be right. For Michael, it is to please other people. He is always the one that organises events for friends and family, turning up with a big smile and gifts under his arm, going out of his way to make sure everyone else is all right, and backing down in arguments when he sees others becoming upset. Michael, however, is very lonely and feels that he always gets overlooked and taken for granted. It is when Michael is by himself that he feels most able to *be* himself.

Changing our way of thinking

Our conditions of worth limit how we think and, as a result, they shape everything we do. They may stop us noticing opportunities or lead us to fail to seize opportunities when we do see them. We need to identify how we talk to ourselves. Say, for example, you are having difficulty finding a new job. What do you say to yourself? Maybe you think it's because they want someone younger. Or perhaps you are finding it difficult in a relationship; maybe you think it is because you are not attractive enough. Each of these examples are ways in which people talk to themselves that ultimately have their roots in their way of thinking about themselves that comes from their conditions of worth. Conditions of worth close us down from thinking openly about situations.

How do we identify when we do this? It is hard because, of course, to us our own explanations seem perfectly sensible. Even if our friends and family try to persuade us otherwise, we don't really hear them. In fact, if they tell us the opposite, we might even laugh it off or swat away their comments in another way.

We are not ready to hear the truth even if it is preferable to what we are telling ourselves. Until we are ready to face the truth, our lives are limited to what our conditions of worth will allow us. Many things happen to us in life that we have no control over, but the one thing that we do have control over is the choices we make. That might sound obvious, but so too is the fact that too often we make bad decisions for ourselves. Sometimes we will make bad decisions because we don't have all the facts, but other times we make bad decisions because we get in our own way by how we approach the facts that we do have. Do we approach life guided by our inner wisdom or are we making decisions on the basis of our conditions of worth?

As a psychotherapist, I have spent many hours listening to clients talking about the misfortunes in their life. At the start of psychotherapy people often tell me their life story. Often, people see themselves as the powerless victims of fate, buffeted by circumstances, struggling against incompetent work colleagues, surrounded by thoughtless relatives and manipulated by forces outside their control. Nothing much will ever happen in psychotherapy until the person wakes up to the fact that in the midst of it all they always have a choice about how to respond. Some people never do, and they remain victims of their own powerless stories, but others get to the point where they suddenly come alive as they realise that no one but themselves can save them from the trap of their own stories.

CASE STUDY: *Jon*

Jon was a client in his forties who was angry with his parents, dissatisfied with his marriage, unhappy at work and, after weeks of telling me about how other people were to blame for the misfortunes in his life, he turned to me and said, 'I am so tired of this. It's all bullshit isn't it?

What I've been saying. It's me isn't it? I need to step up and take some responsibility.'

Everything began to change for Jon after that. It wasn't easy by any means. But now that he no longer saw himself as the powerless victim but as someone who could begin to shape his own life, he could begin to think seriously about how to deal with his marriage problems and issues at work.

Moving on through understanding what drives us

Sometimes a person's conditions of worth can propel them to great success. But because conditions of worth arise from other people's dreams and expectations and not our own, they do not always align well with our natural talents, interests and abilities. It might be that we end up struggling to be a success at something that we are not a good fit for. And we look to others to tell us how well we are doing rather than learning to evaluate our competence for ourselves. As a result, conditions of worth are more likely to lead to a life of unhappiness and a lack of fulfilment and true excellence, even if other forms of success also come their way.

Once we have identified our own conditions of worth we can begin to understand what drives us, and when we know ourselves that bit better we can begin to make wiser decisions. When our lives are governed by our conditions of worth we don't know our own truths. We don't know what it is that deep down we want to say yes to. The key to overcoming our conditions of worth is first to understand them and how they form a block to self-acceptance. How can we accept ourselves if we continue judging ourselves by some rules that we took on board years ago that have become so deep-seated within us that we don't even recognise them for what they are – the voices of others that drown out our own inner voice of wisdom?

While those old voices dominate us, we can't change until we begin to learn self-acceptance and the ability to relate to ourselves unconditionally. Until we face up to ourselves just as we are, with our strengths and weaknesses, we will remain stuck, repeating past patterns. For Rogers, the key to human growth was self-acceptance. He said, 'The curious paradox is that when I accept myself just as I am, then I can change.'

We need to unlock our conditions of worth

Many people simply do not learn to be able to nurture themselves, and they constantly need others around them to give them their sense of worth.

CASE STUDY: *Rory*

Rory had done well at school but he had fallen into his career path because of a suggestion from his father to go into banking. Looking back, he says that banking didn't actually interest him that much, but in his family it was seen as important to be successful in life, and that meant earning a high salary and living in an expensive house with top-of-the-range cars parked in the drive. He remembers the conversation with his father about which university course to attend and his father's comment that business and finance were where the money was but, even as he filled in the forms for college, he thought that he didn't want to study business. Now, all these years later, he is living a life that is the consequence of that evening.

Now successful in banking and earning a very high salary, he has fulfilled his ambitions, but he is deeply unhappy. His father instilled in him the importance of making money, so you would expect that he would now have his father's approval. He hasn't: just before Rory got his big break in banking, his father lost his own money in the banking crash. Rory's father, instead of giving his son the approval he so wanted, is now resentful of his son's success. In this way, Rory has spent his adult life striving for his father's approval never to achieve it. He has no ability to accept himself and feels trapped, lonely and deeply unhappy, as each and everything he does he looks to others for approval.

If we can free ourselves from our conditions of worth, we can more readily learn to be ourselves. Take ten minutes to try the following exercise.

EXERCISE: What qualities do you feel you need to be valued?

How would you complete the following sentence? Just quickly say what comes to mind:

'If I am to be of value, I must _____'

What phrase did you come up with? Typically, when asked to complete the sentence above people say things like:

- Work hard
- Please others
- Never cry
- Not get angry
- Never let others see weakness
- Do as I am told
- Be strong

- Be clever
- Be silent
- Be small
- Be the best
- Always be right
- Always win
- Be perfect
- Be beautiful
- Be successful
- Be wealthy

The chances are that one of these is close to the phrase you came up with. Write your phrase down and place it in front of you. Now just let whatever memories, thoughts and feelings you have enter your mind. Just observe whatever comes to mind for a minute. Then, in a notebook, write down a description of what came to mind and how you felt about it. Let the words flow onto the page and just write whatever comes to mind without censoring yourself.

———————

When we are locked into conditions of worth, we need constant approval from others that we are working hard enough, earning enough, being the best, or whatever it is that we feel we need to do to meet their expectations and be valued. But no matter how hard we try to get their approval to satisfy our inner critical voices, it will never truly satisfy because what we really need is self-approval. Until we are able to accept ourselves as we are, our inner critical voices will continue to haunt us by saying such things as:

- I am bad
- I am worthless
- I am unlikeable
- I am defective

- I am repulsive
- I am useless
- I am stupid
- I am inferior

The power of the authenticity formula is recognising that it is not enough simply to try to be ourselves. We also need to know ourselves and own ourselves. If we attempt to be ourselves without first knowing ourselves, the danger is that we will simply mistake these critical voices for our inner voice of wisdom. The point is to learn to recognise your conditions of worth and how they are at the root of your negative self-talk so that you begin to take control of how you talk to yourself and how you present yourself to others.

We carry the baggage of our conditions of worth

Our conditions of worth are forged in childhood when we are vulnerable to the influences of those around us. As we enter adulthood we are no longer vulnerable to these influences, but nonetheless we often carry on as if we were. Without being aware of what we are doing we may even seek out new relationships that reinforce our conditions of worth, as that is what we know. Most of all we are likely to have failed to learn to trust our own inner voice of wisdom, so drawn are we to the need for others' approval.

In the story of the Wizard of Oz, Dorothy, the Tin Man, the Scarecrow and the Lion defeat the wicked witch and return to the Emerald City. The Great Wizard has promised to grant their wishes if they defeat the witch. Dorothy hopes to return to Kansas, the Tin Man desires a heart, the Lion, courage and the Scarecrow, brains. Cowering before the booming voice of the Wizard, Dorothy and her chums ask him to fulfil his promise. But, by accident, the curtain falls away.

The Wizard is revealed as a small old man speaking into

a megaphone and pulling frantically at levers. It is all smoke and mirrors. The Wizard realises that his deception has been revealed. 'I'm not a bad man, just a bad wizard,' he says. But Dorothy's chums insist he keeps his promise. The Wizard presents the Scarecrow with a certificate, the Tin Man with a clock and the Lion with medals. He is a wise man who knows that the human qualities of brains, heart and courage cannot be given. As such, he offers his gifts allegorically. In giving these gifts he acknowledges that, through their trials and tribulations, what Dorothy's companions are seeking was always within themselves. During their adventures, the Scarecrow had admirably shown his brains, the Tin Man his heart and the Lion his bravery. Not realising that the gifts are only allegorical, Dorothy's chums dance with delight.

Too often, we act like tin men, scarecrows and cowardly lions, expecting others to provide the solutions to our difficulties. But, as this allegorical tale shows us, the solutions are actually within us. Other people cannot tell us what meanings to make or what directions we should take in our lives. That has to come from us. We have to learn to listen carefully to ourselves and not let our own voices be drowned out by others.

If we become wise to our conditions of worth and how they prevent us from listening to our inner voice of wisdom we can begin to counter these influences from the past. One way we can do this is to seek out relationships in which we are accepted for who we are.

Loving relationships continue to matter

We have seen how loving relationships are the key to our personal development and growth as young people, as they support our needs for agency and belonging and allow us to find our own best directions in life.

The importance of such relationships continue throughout our lives into adulthood. To be our best we need empathic, genuine and unconditionally supportive relationships: people who cherish us as we are and inspire us to be our best.

Good relationships provide us with intimacy where we feel free to express ourselves and in which we feel understood, validated and cared for. Decades of research show that intimate human relationships help us flourish. When our basic needs for agency and belonging are satisfied in our relationships – be they at work, with family or friends – greater well-being results. Happier people report greater levels of social participation, they are more likely to feel that they have friends to count on and they trust others, view their relationships more positively and spend less time alone and more time with family, friends or romantic partners.

Poor-quality relationships or the lack of such caring relationships are associated with the presence of mental-health difficulties. People with problems of depression and anxiety tend to have less intimate, less confiding, less responsive and more conflictual relationships, they also have less contact with friends and, in many cases, they lack close relationships.

Distress related to interpersonal problems is one of the main reasons that clients come to psychotherapy or counselling. At least part of the healing power of therapy is down to the ability of a good therapist to offer an empathic, genuine and unconditional relationship that can meet the person's needs for agency and belonging. In such a relationship, we feel safe to get to know ourselves and explore behind the mask that we may be wearing. Talking our lives through openly and honestly with another person can be helpful because it reduces the psychological tension of inauthenticity and the stress upon us from the act of self-concealment.[42]

As we explore within ourselves, we become aware of the feelings and experiences that we have suppressed. We learn about ourselves and what we truly want out of our lives. Good therapists help us to challenge our perceptions and be open to new perspectives, and through their acceptance of us we will learn to be accepting of ourselves.[43]

Unfortunately, all too often we lack empathic, genuine and unconditional relationships that help to deflate and counter our conditions of worth, so we continue to accept ourselves only conditionally.

Seek out positive relationships

We should strive to be unconditionally accepting, genuine and empathic in our relationships with others and we might hope that we get the same back; however, although we might deeply desire positive relationships in which we are accepted for who we are and are able to be ourselves, it is not what we always have. Toxic relationships are those that are conditional, lack empathy and are less than genuine. Be they family relationships or those we have at work, the stark reality of what most of us have to contend with is relationships that we are only too glad to escape from. It might be the relief of leaving home to get to work or the relief of leaving work to get home, or, sadly for many of us, the in-between ground of the car when we have the solitude of being alone.

Positive relationships are worth striving for, but it might be that there are occasions when being on our own is a better option that gives us the space in our lives to seek out new relationships that better meet our needs.

It takes a huge amount of energy to maintain a sense of self within a toxic relationship that is based on conditions of worth. We have to invest energy into psychological defences to prevent us from finding out the truth about ourselves.

Authentic people have minimal defences. They are open to experience and, as such, they are always learning about themselves. They are able to look at themselves honestly, not only at what they are good at but also at their flaws, imperfections and mistakes. They can be critical of their behaviour, not to put themselves down but to learn and to change. They can be critical of one aspect of their behaviour without generalising this to themselves as a whole. They recognise that as a human being they will make mistakes. They recognise that it makes no sense to compare our overall worth as human beings with other people, but they recognise instead that different people have different strengths, talents and abilities but are all equal as human beings. In short, authentic people approach the world without making overgeneralisations. They have a flexible mindset that weighs up the reality of any given situation and promotes constructive action to be taken.

In the next chapter I will look at how people often defend themselves from the truth as a way to maintain the conditional picture they have of themselves. You may be surprised at the complexities of how people defend themselves. You may even have a light-bulb moment as you recognise yourself in some of the descriptions.

Chapter 5

Spot Your Defences

Every day you will encounter defensive behaviours either within yourself or in other people. Until we are able to spot our own defences we will continue to be controlled by them to the detriment of ourselves and our relationships.

According to Freud,[44] who introduced the notion of defence mechanisms, we use defence mechanisms to reduce anxious feelings. Anxiety is uncomfortable, but it serves an important purpose. Anxiety acts as the body's warning system. In a sense, it is like a smoke detector. A smoke detector tells us that something is burning and gives us time to react. We can switch the toaster off or, in more extreme circumstances, get out of the building in time before the fire spreads.

In the same way, anxious feelings sound a warning that something isn't right. Anxiety keeps us on our toes to avoid danger and help us to prevent future difficulties. Walking home late at night along a quiet road in an unfamiliar area, it is natural to feel some anxiety. We feel more awake, alert to our surroundings and ready for action. For this reason we do well to not ignore anxiety and what steps we need to take.

It makes good sense to be alert to anxiety, but, going back

to the smoke detector analogy, let me ask you a question: have you ever taken the batteries out of a smoke detector to make it stop? Many of us have and, of course, that's often what we do with anxious feelings too, we try to shut them off. When there is real physical danger that we don't deal with, we soon suffer the consequences; however, when our anxiety is not caused by an objectively threatening event in the world but by the niggling discomfort that comes with the psychological tension of living inauthentically, we can take the batteries out and, on the face of it, nothing bad immediately happens. In this way we are able to suppress our tension of living inauthentically for months, perhaps years and maybe even entire lifetimes, without realising we are even doing so.

A defence mechanism is a strategy, unconsciously used, largely involuntary and often learned in childhood, that arises to protect ourselves from psychological danger. People cope with the anxiety produced when they feel threatened, unsafe, unloved and unvalued by disowning their real feelings and turning instead to elaborate defensive strategies. Defences can help us in the short term to manage difficult situations and emotions that may otherwise overwhelm us. However, when used consistently, they begin to create problems as they distort, transform or falsify reality.

We distort, transform and falsify reality as a defence mechanism

Defence mechanisms are a way of understanding how people cloud themselves from reality.[45] Because of defence mechanisms, we sometimes behave in ways that we ourselves simply do not understand.

It was Freud who originally developed the idea of defences, but it was his daughter Anna Freud who extended her father's ideas. Anna was the last of Sigmund Freud's six children, born in 1895 in Vienna. She became a psychoanalyst in her own right. In 1936 she published her most well-known book, *The Ego and the Mechanisms of Defence*, in which she described the different forms of defence that people use to ward off anxiety.

Defence mechanisms are all too real and used by all of us, at least sometimes, but for some they become habitual, overused and the barrier against authenticity.

Defence mechanisms that deny

Psychologists have observed that some defence mechanisms seem to have their roots in childhood. These are the immature defence mechanisms – so called because they are favoured especially by children.[46] Imagine a child covering their eyes thinking that by so doing you cannot see them. Throughout life, many adults who don't learn better ways of coping will continue to resort to these immature defences that deny reality. It is to these that we will now turn. The first and most basic of the defence mechanisms to develop is denial.

CASE STUDY: *Paul*

Paul lost his wife to cancer. But rather than face the painful feelings that were evoked in him, his friends and family were surprised by how he took a matter-of-fact attitude and carried on as if he were unaffected. Friends and family thought it strange that he was behaving in such a way and thought him cold and unloving when in fact the very opposite was the case. The loss of his wife was simply too much for him to bear.

Denial is the refusal to accept reality and is an extreme form of self-protection. The person acts as if a painful event, thought or feeling simply had not happened. They behave in a way that suggests they do not know something that they would be expected to know. Denial is considered one of the earliest defence mechanisms, because it is characteristic of childhood, as described above when young children cover their eyes believing that you can't see them. How strange to think that as adults we continue to use denial in our everyday lives to avoid dealing with painful feelings or areas of our life that we don't wish to face up to. We make meaning of events in such a way so that any threat disappears.

For Paul, denial helped him deal with the loss of his wife. In the short term, denial can be helpful, but in the longer term, if it prevents us from working through emotional issues, it can be harmful. Survivors of traumatic events often experience a period of denial in the initial aftermath, which helps them to cope, but if there is too much denial for too long, they are likely to suffer from problems later.[47] As long as you deny the reality of your experience, whatever it is that is crying out to be worked through will not be and it will come back to bite you, sometimes with devastating consequences.

CASE STUDY: *Mary*

Mary would often have a few glasses of wine in the evening after work, even if she was driving. Her husband would point out to her that she was taking risks, and arguments would often ensue between them, as Mary simply denied that she had a problem or that her driving was affected. One evening, Mary drove them both to a restaurant where she ordered a glass of wine. Mark was annoyed and pointed out to her that as it was her turn to drive she shouldn't have anything to drink. The meal continued in stony silence. Mary ordered a second glass as she finished her first. Mark gave her a look to say you really shouldn't be doing this. Mary became offended by Mark's expression. She believed that having another glass of wine was harmless and that Mark was being unreasonable.

As you can imagine, the rest of the evening continued in silence until they arrived home, when they had a blazing argument.

Not surprisingly, a few months later, Mary was stopped by the police after causing an accident while under the influence of alcohol. Mary was shocked by what had happened. She was arrested and spent the night in police custody. In talking to her I realised that despite Mark's protestations Mary really did not know she was breaking the law or even that she was doing anything dangerous. She had completely blocked this fact from her awareness. When she was convicted a month later and lost her driving licence, the reality of the situation hit her like a blow to the head. She was absolutely stunned by her own behaviour. 'How did I not know what I was doing?' It was only the experience of being convicted for driving under the influence of alcohol and the fear of prison that jolted Mary out of her denial.

Splitting is another mechanism that develops early on in life. Instead of seeing the complexities of life, children will see things in black and white, as good or bad, or as right or wrong, allowing them to begin to make sense of the world in a primitive way.

As adults, we can revert back to splitting in difficult situations.

CASE STUDY: *Robin*

Robin's marriage has had its ups and downs ever since he and Shazia got married ten years ago. Days, weeks, even months go by and all is well, but then, following a disagreement, Robin will fly into a rage and shut himself off, expressing concerns about his marriage and threatening divorce. When Robin talks about the situations that lead to this, the first thing that strikes me is that more often than not the disagreements are over the most trivial events, such as Shazia being late home from work not having made it clear to him in advance that she was going out with friends that evening. It's not that Robin is possessive, although it certainly sounds like that, but rather when confronted by stress he switches into viewing his marriage in black-and-white terms. It is either the best or the worst. Shazia is either the most loving and considerate person in the world or she is the most spiteful and uncaring. There is no middle ground for Robin, so he oscillates between extreme positions.

Repression The essence of repression lies in not allowing dangerous, unacceptable thoughts, feelings and impulses to enter our consciousness. Take, for example, failing to recognise our sexual attraction to a colleague of the same gender if we are heterosexual. Understandably, we might want to repress things about ourselves that we perceive as unsettling, inadequate or shameful. In a culture in which homosexuality is still perceived by many as something to be ashamed of, it is not surprising that some men and women will repress their true feelings. Repression can be used to keep from knowing ourselves. There are many things that we often don't want to face up to. Who wants to know that they are not as attractive as they think, as talented, as intelligent, as popular or whatever other knowledge of ourselves that we sweep under our mental carpet?

Keep in mind that repression might work to keep such knowledge from ourselves, but it might not prevent others from perceiving the reality of our situation. Repression requires constant expenditure of psychological energy, as the repressed material seeks to find an outlet. In Freudian thought, psychosomatic ailments or other psychological problems may have their roots in repression.

CASE STUDY: *Toni*

Toni has not had sexual relations with her husband for over a year. She would like to, but her husband is no longer interested because of a medical condition and has moved into a different bedroom. Dealing with the frustration is difficult for Toni, and it is noticeable that she has taken up smoking cigarettes again after having quit for a number of years. Cigarettes have become Toni's outlet for her repressed sexual energy. For others it could be working long hours, intense sporting activities, or long periods in the gym.

Sublimation is simply the channelling of unacceptable impulses, thoughts and emotions into more acceptable ones. For instance, when a person has sexual impulses they do not want to act upon, they may instead focus on rigorous exercise or immerse themselves in work. Often, sexual or aggressive energy, which cannot find an appropriate outlet, is turned towards intellectual, artistic or cultural expression. Sublimation is referred to as a mature defence in comparison to the immature defences we have looked at already. It has even been referred to as the successful defence, insofar as the energy is diverted into other constructive outlets.

Defence mechanisms that distort reality

As we age, we tend to develop other more complex mechanisms that twist and distort the truth.

Projection is when we attribute to another person motivations, feelings and thoughts that are actually our own but we are unable to see these in ourselves.

For Mark and Mary, it was Mark who became angry at Mary for not listening, but in actual fact *he* was not listening to *her*. If he had been, he may have understood better how Mary was stressed at work, and her use of alcohol was a way of coping that had become habitual. She wasn't drinking to annoy him, but she actually did not understand the situation. Perhaps, if Mark had been more attentive and listened to Mary, she might have been able to be less defensive and open to realising the danger she was putting herself in.

Projection is another immature mechanism, often the result of a lack of insight and acknowledgement of one's own motivations and feelings. Mark lacked the self-knowledge to know what he was doing, and projection was a well-used defence for him in other areas of his life. He often accuses others of not listening to him, but in fact he is a poor listener himself. Another example of projection is illustrated by Ben's case study.

CASE STUDY: *Ben*

As a senior executive in a large company, Ben is proud of his job. If you met him at a party, it wouldn't be long before he would be telling you about his important position. After university he spent 15 years dedicated to advancing his career before landing his dream appointment. But now, three years on, he is struggling. Despite his ambition, he lacks the necessary leadership skills to fulfil his duties. His inability to listen well is one of the major problems he has, and his staff often complain among themselves that they don't feel heard by him. It is clear to everyone except Ben that he is out of his depth. How can he not see this for himself when it is so obvious to others? Ben does what many of us do when faced with a threat to our self-image: he blames other people. He blames his subordinates for not being competent enough to provide him with the information he needs. He blames his superiors for not taking the correct decisions to steer his projects in the right direction in the first place, when in fact it is his own lack of competence that is the issue.

Blaming other people is a sure-fire way of maintaining our self-image when we are under threat. Most of us, at one time or another, will point the blame at others for our own failings, but after a few hours or days we will admit to ourselves what really happened. It might be a blow to our self-image, but we learn from our experience. We gain in self-knowledge, change our image of ourselves and become more realistic – and in this way we are able to navigate the world better. But this is not what Ben does.

Instead of accommodating new information into an ever-changing self-image, Ben has become a master of self-deception to ensure that his self-image doesn't change. He attributes to others the characteristics that he possesses but which are unacceptable to his conscious awareness. Not surprisingly, Ben was always finding himself at loggerheads with his staff and with senior management. Friends, who only ever heard his side of the story over dinner, would listen aghast to his tales of mismanagement and bungling and wonder how the company kept afloat. Little did they know that it was Ben's account of himself that was grossly distorted. Projection is used especially when we find the thoughts unacceptable to us. The main thing about projection is that we do not see in ourselves the faults that we think are obvious in others.

Dissociation Another way of distorting reality is through dissociation. Dissociation is when a person loses track of time or themselves and their usual thought processes. They may feel disconnected from themselves in their world; for example, if we are driving and we suddenly realise that we have no recollection of the past ten minutes, we would have been in a dissociated state. Mark and Mary appeared for couples counselling, but it was clear that when Mary was explaining how she felt about their situation, Mark wasn't listening. In fact sometimes, as the conversation became ever more stressful between them, it was like he would enter a different state of consciousness. It seemed like Mark wasn't even present in his body.

Rationalisation Another immature mechanism is rationalisation. This is when we give socially acceptable reasons for behaviour that is based on unacceptable motives: for example, when we are not offered that dream job, but we then tell ourselves and others that we didn't really want it anyway or that actually what was important was the experience of the interview itself. It's not simply that we are telling people this, but that we come to believe it ourselves. Such rationalisations may disguise our fear and lack of self-esteem.

Regression refers to reversion to an earlier stage of development when we are confronted with unacceptable thoughts or feelings.

In the arguments between Mary and her husband about her drinking, Mark would often become so angry that Mary wasn't listening to his warning that he would storm off and sulk like a child. Such behaviour was characteristic of Mark. One evening in a restaurant, the food was late in being served. To Mary's embarrassment, Mark began to lose his temper. He shouted at the waiter and pounded his fist on the table. Mary later described it as like being out with a toddler.

That is a more extreme example, but there are lots of behaviours that we engage in that we probably don't think of as regression. I know when I've had a hard week and I am feeling in need of some comfort, I like to spend the afternoon on the couch watching some old favourite Westerns from my childhood. Regressive behaviours are so common that we don't even recognise them as such, so much of our behaviour is regressive in the ways we revert to childish patterns.

Advertisers and marketers know this all too well as they watch us pushing our trolleys around supermarkets stocking up on childish comforts. We sink into our sofas watching programmes suitable for children that remind us of the safety of our own childhoods, with pizza and ice cream, as a way of fending off the anxiety from an increasingly uncertain and terrifying world.

Acting out is when we perform extreme behaviours as a way to express thoughts or feelings that we feel incapable of otherwise expressing. During one evening meal together when Mark became upset with Mary, he threw his plate of food onto the floor.

Displacement is when we redirect thoughts, feelings and impulses from one person or object towards another; for example, our boss is angry with us at work, but we hold back from responding until we get home, when we shout at the children. We use displacement when we cannot express our feelings safely, then when we are in a situation where we can give vent to our feelings we do so, but the target of our venting is no longer appropriate.

Reaction formation is when we show characteristics that are the opposite of our true selves, such as in the case study below.

CASE STUDY: *Vic/Victoria*

Vic was always the first to suggest a game of poker after hours, when the pubs had shut, and he was always the most competitive and aggressive at play. All his friends would have described him as quite 'macho'. Not for a second did anyone suspect that, ten years later, Vic would live in Australia and go by the name of Victoria. For years, Victoria had fended off her inner discomfort by behaving in an excessively masculine way. On moving to Australia and leaving her old life behind, Victoria was able to live a life consistent with her true self.

Undoing is the attempt to take back an unconscious behaviour or thought that is unacceptable or hurtful; for example, most of us can recall a time when we have said something to someone unintentionally that insulted them, at which point we go into reverse gear and spend the next hour praising them for their attractiveness, intellect, or whatever it was that we insulted, in an attempt to counteract the damage done by the original comment. If you have ever found yourself in that situation, you may have found yourself thinking: *I'm making things worse*, but somehow you keep on going, trying to undo the situation.

Defence mechanisms that can be useful

Defence mechanisms can cause us problems, because they twist, distort and transform reality, but it is important to acknowledge that, occasionally, they can also be useful in getting us through challenging times. As we have already seen in the case of denial or sublimation, they can lead us to engage in behaviours that are useful in other ways. Other defence mechanisms that can also be useful include intellectualisation, humour and identification.

Intellectualisation is when we override our emotions with thinking as a way to deal with an unacceptable impulse, situation or behaviour: for example, a person who has just been given a terminal medical diagnosis might focus on the details of medical procedures in a seemingly cold and calm way, to the surprise of those around him, but this is their way of managing the situation.

Humour is another example when used as a mature defence mechanism. The channelling of unacceptable impulses or thoughts into a light-hearted story or joke can help people cope. The use of black humour is typical in those such as emergency-service workers who routinely deal with loss and tragedy on a daily basis.

Identification Another way that can get us through difficult situations is identification. Identification is the opposite of projection. Rather than attributing one's own thoughts and feelings to another, we take on the values and feelings of the other person as our own. An extreme example is people held in captivity who adopt the behaviours and attitudes of their persecutors. In some situations this might just work in helping us to survive an otherwise challenging situation. It is one of the things that children do that can help them get through a violent upbringing, but as we saw in the previous chapters, while it might help in the moment it sets the scene for problems later in life.

So much more is going on under the surface in our everyday interactions than we usually acknowledge. As we have seen, defence mechanisms can, for short periods of time, be useful. When an upsetting situation could potentially overwhelm us, our defences can allow us to keep going. In other cases, they allow us to channel our energies into more productive behaviours when there is no other outlet. Ultimately, however, a reliance on defences for prolonged periods of time is to live our lives in darkness because they do not help us learn from experiences. Defences distort and twist reality for us in ways that provide a roadblock to authentic living.

Limiting our defences for an authentic life

One aim of this book is to help you relinquish your defences which alienate you from your true likes and dislikes, hopes, fears and desires, so that you can get in touch with the real you. Defences are the opposite of authenticity. These are the various ways in which we defend ourselves from the reality of our thoughts, feelings and the situation around us. Remember, defence mechanisms are most often learned behaviours. We learned to protect ourselves during childhood. The chances are that these were helpful things that we learned to do that got us through difficult situations. It is important to understand that such behaviours have a reason and once may have served us well. But, as adults, we can choose to learn some new behaviours and move towards becoming more open to experience.

In reading the above, a few of the things that you do might have come to mind as you recognised yourself in some of the examples.

All of the above defences are ways of avoiding reality, excluding reality, repackaging reality, reversing or redirecting reality, although they can be useful in some circumstances in helping us to protect ourselves from being flooded with anxiety which can cause us other difficulties. In this way, some use of self-deception may at times be useful to us.

In general, we carry around with us a variety of illusions that shield us from reality and which allow us to be more optimistic about the future than is justified, thereby helping us to feel better about ourselves.[48] It is possible to see that in some situations, for a period of time, the use of defences can get us through those otherwise difficult times. We need to be able to respect each other's use of defences knowing that it's the best that we can do in that moment to cope. But at the same time we need to know that, in the longer run, the continual use of defences will lead to problems and most of all they will prevent us from the joy and freedom of living an authentic life. A little bit of self-deception at times might do little harm, but in the long run, and when it comes to serious issues in our lives, failing to confront reality is not the way to a flourishing life.

Through the use of these various defences, we are stopped from knowing ourselves, we prevent ourselves from realistically appraising our part in shaping the events that befall us and they get in our own way when it comes to making good decisions. We do this in the name of hanging on to our inauthentic selves – selves that we have worked hard to develop over many years in response to the pressures on us to conform and belong. But one thing that psychologists know is that you can only keep the truth down for so long. The more defensive we are in our lives, the more difficulties will unfold for us, and the more we will be plagued by discomfort, anxiety and the niggling sense that things are not quite right.

Be open to learning from your experiences

Too often, when we are faced with difficult situations, we avoid them, whether it is arguments with work colleagues or difficult meetings, we try not to think about them. We get home from work and turn on the television, pour a glass of wine, or perhaps we take out our frustrations in the gym or on the PlayStation. Whatever we do, it is likely to be the opposite of looking forward to the next argument or the next meeting. But, in fact, that's what we need to do to learn about ourselves.

One of the most common occasions when we can see our defences at play is when we get unsolicited advice and criticism from others. It might be a colleague at work giving us some friendly advice on how to do a task better next time, or a friend who wants to tell us something that will be helpful to us although it is painful to hear. Perhaps it is a family member trying to work through a disagreement with us. We might like to think that we can take criticism, but actually most of us are not that good at it. Often, when we hear what sounds like criticism, our defences immediately go up. We take aim and bat the criticism away to the boundary. We wheel out our defence mechanisms of blaming other people, making jokes, getting angry, becoming indignant and all the other myriad ways we avoid hearing what's being said. The point of defence mechanisms like these is, of course, that we don't know that's what we are doing. We are literally defending ourselves from the truth about ourselves.

It might be easier to see this happening in other people than ourselves. There are people who are prickly and hard to get near; some who quickly become distraught at the hint of a challenge. There are others who are so slippery that talking to them is like chasing a bar of soap around the bath.

There are times and places when we might want to avoid a challenge. The trouble comes when we don't know that we are using defensive strategies. We are the person who can't take the truth. When confronted by challenging new information, it's always worth listening and trying to hear if there is any truth behind it. The fact is we probably don't know ourselves as well as we think we do. Next time, rather than immediately batting criticism away, ask yourself: is there anything in this that might be useful to me? If we can do this, we are always open to change. And when we are open to change we constantly grow as people, becoming wiser and more able to navigate the world and our relationships. The first step is to stop the next time you find yourself reaching for your bat, put it down and ask yourself: is there any truth to this, even just a tiny bit? Learn to listen, sort the useful information from the rest and let the useful information in. As painful as the truth might be in the short term, the benefits of knowing yourself better will follow.

For Carl Rogers, whom we met in the previous chapter, the most important characteristic of the fully functioning life was not feeling good but being open to processing information about ourselves in an unbiased way.[49] In everyday life, we are confronted with situations that threaten our self-image; for example, when we fail at a task at work or when we say something inappropriate to someone we love and thereby cause an argument. The truth is that we often find some way of not taking responsibility for our mistakes – we blame others, refuse to admit our failings, and so on. We use our psychological defences to stop ourselves hearing the truth. Authentic people are open to experience and cherish the challenges of learning about themselves.

If we can transform our anxiety into an enthusiasm to engage with the challenge and learn from it, we are on our way to authenticity.

PART II

Why Authenticity Matters

*Happiness is when what you think, what you
say and what you do are in harmony*

Mohandas Gandhi

In the following chapters we will look at why authenticity
matters and the recent work of positive psychologists, who
have taken up the challenges of putting authenticity under the
spotlight of research. Their findings show how authentic living
benefits our well-being.

Chapter 6

The Flourishing Life

Positive psychology was formally launched by Martin Seligman in his presidential address to the American Psychological Association in 1998. Seligman said how the idea of positive psychology came to him following a moment of epiphany when gardening with his daughter, Nikki, who was then aged five, when she instructed him not to be such a grouch. 'In that moment, I acquired the mission of helping to build the scientific infrastructure of a field that would investigate what makes life worth living: positive emotion, positive character and positive institutions.'[1] What Seligman realised was that when it comes to understanding problems in living, a considerable amount of time and money had been spent over the years documenting the various ways in which people suffer psychologically, but nowhere near the same effort had gone into understanding what makes life worth living. Seligman resolved to use his presidency to initiate a shift in psychology's focus towards a more positive psychology.

Since these beginnings, positive psychology has attracted worldwide interest.[2] But the most notable achievement of positive psychology has been its attempt to look again at what it means to have 'a good life'.

Many scholars and philosophers have, of course, considered the question of the good life throughout human history, but positive psychology has opened our minds to the fact that a good life is not defined solely by the absence of psychological problems but by experiences that go above and beyond the absence of problems. The good life also consists of the presence of a range of experiences such as joy, zest, excitement, meaning, purpose and friendship – all the things that make us feel alive and want to get out of bed in the morning. It seems remarkable that until positive psychology so little attention had been paid by psychologists to the good life.

Most had simply assumed that a good life resulted from the absence of psychological problems. But then the realisation began to dawn that the absence of problems was not the same as living a fulfilled, meaningful and happy life. Psychologists began to think about what makes for a good life. Their conclusion echoed that of the humanistic psychologists decades earlier that the most important skills we can learn in life are those that lead us to authentic living.[3]

Achieving the good life through a flowing, changing process

Previously, we met Abraham Maslow, the founder of humanistic psychology, who talked about self-actualisation, and Carl Rogers, the founder of counselling, who talked about people becoming fully functioning. Maslow and Rogers used different terms, but they were essentially referring to the Aristotelian idea of eudaimonia, as I explained in Chapter 2.[4]

Positive psychology is also inspired by the Aristotelian model of human nature. Individuals are characterised by experiencing joy when exercising their inherent or acquired abilities and striving towards realising them in ways that are experienced as better, more complex or more perfect. The Aristotelian model holds that development of any organism, including human beings, is the unfolding of natural, fixed or innate potentialities. The good life is when we are free to flourish.

As before, we can use the metaphor of how an acorn has within it all the instructions it needs to become an oak tree. An acorn does not become a dog or a cat; it becomes an oak tree. All biological life could be seen as driven by this single principle of achieving the best of its inherent nature. Birds are destined to fly and spiders to weave webs. It is human nature that children become adults who walk, talk, listen, think, create, investigate, build, sing, dance and draw, and do all the other things that make us human. There are things that characteristically make us human, and each of us has his or her own unique strengths, talents and abilities. To be the best we are, and to be most truly ourselves, means to develop these potentials to their full.

We are always striving to realise our potentialities more and more. For Carl Rogers, the good life was not a fixed, unchanging state of happiness and contentment, but rather it could be seen as a flowing, changing process. He wrote:

> The good life is a process, not a state of being ... It is a direction, not a destination. The direction ... is that which is selected by the total organism, when there is psychological freedom to move in any direction.[5]

Rogers's view was that the good life is not an outcome to be achieved, once and for all, but rather it is a process that we are constantly engaged with and are continually moving towards when we are the authors of our own lives. Rogers described the directions taken by people as they become more fully functioning. These include movement:

- Away from façades
- Away from oughts
- Away from meeting expectations
- Away from pleasing others

- Towards self-direction
- Towards openness to experience
- Towards acceptance of others
- Towards trusting oneself

In these ways we become free to move in a new direction that is most authentic to us.[6]

Picking up where Rogers left off, modern-day positive psychologists have begun to look deeper into eudaimonia as a process.

Orientations to life: the reasons behind what you do

One psychologist who has pioneered research into eudaimonic psychology is Veronika Huta at the University of Ottawa.[7] Huta says that the differences between the eudaimonic and hedonic life are seen in people's orientations to life, that is to say their whys of what they do. The *eudaimonically oriented* person values personal growth, seeks new challenges, strives for excellence in what they do and looks for meaningful purpose in their life. They set goals for themselves that are intrinsically valuable to them and part of their identity. In contrast, the *hedonically oriented* person seeks pleasure, enjoyment, comfort or relaxation.

Because their orientations are different, they have contrasting behaviours and experiences. The eudaimonic person is more likely to engage in activities such as volunteering, donating money and time to those less fortunate, and taking part in worthwhile political and charitable causes. They also tend more towards expressing gratitude, being mindful and taking part in challenging activities that demand they apply their skills and talents in such a way as to provide a sense of meaning and purpose – and they become deeply engaged in their work and leisure activities.

The hedonic person likes going to parties, attending sporting events and concerts. They focus more on immediate pleasure.

In short, whereas hedonia refers to the pleasures of life – what we seek when we sit down in front of the television with a pizza – eudaimonism refers to effortfully engaging in activities that express our essential selves and that give us a sense of meaning and purpose. Of course, in most cases, people's lives contain a mixture of eudaimonic and hedonic orientations, although some are more weighted towards one than the other.

EXERCISE: Think about the balance of your intentions

The following exercise asks you to rate the extent to which you approach life with either eudaimonic or hedonic intentions.

Please read the two descriptions below. Which one is more like you? If you think only the description on the left sounds like you, then give yourself a 1. If you think only the description on the right sounds like you, then give yourself a 7. Or you may feel that you are somewhere in the middle of the two descriptions. Give yourself a 4 if you think you have the perfect balance between the two.

I am the sort of person who is always looking for opportunities where I can just chill out, have fun, and enjoy myself.	I am the sort of person who is always looking for opportunities to learn new things, gain wisdom, and help others.
I am much more like this	I am much more like this

1   2   3   4   5   6   7

Are you more hedonically or eudaimonically orientated? Do you think you have the right balance of the two orientations in your life?

The conclusion is that pleasure without purpose feels empty, but, ironically, when we feel empty of purpose we tend to chase pleasure even more as a way to fill the void.

For many of us this will sound all too familiar when we think of our own lives and how we manage to deal with the times when we feel empty. Sitting on the sofa eating crisps and watching television will ultimately not compensate for a life where you are not following passion and purpose.

But do your intentions actually reflect how you spend your time?

EXERCISE: How do you spend your time?

Think about how you spend your time. Try setting your watch or mobile phone to bleep at ten random points during the day for the next few days. As it bleeps, make a note of what you are doing at that time. Are you working? Are you spending time with friends? Are you sitting reading? Whatever it might be that you are doing, just make a note. Are you are doing something that is hedonic or eudaimonic in orientation? Why are you doing what you are doing? Dig deep into the reason; for example, you might say, 'I am working.' Why? 'Because I need the money.' Why? 'To be able to look after my family.' Why? 'Because my family give me meaning in life.' Search for the reason, beyond which there is no further reason for why you do what you do.

Work out the balance for yourself between your time spent on hedonic versus eudaimonic activity. Ultimately, the good life must also involve the eudaimonic orientation.

The health benefits of eudaimonia

A study led by Barbara Fredrickson at the University of North Carolina showed that eudaimonic well-being provides cellular health benefits over and above hedonic well-being.[8] The researchers found that eudaimonic well-being was associated with greater antiviral responses, which are associated with better health. However, this was not the case for hedonic well-being, which Fredrickson likened to 'empty calories'. Just as we can enjoy an unhealthy meal with no nutritional value, so too can we find pleasures in life that make us happy, but at the cellular level our bodies appear to respond better to well-being that is based on authenticity, personal growth and purpose in life.

If eudaimonic well-being has such a profound effect at the cellular level, then it probably has considerable benefits for psychological health, too.

Michael Steger and colleagues asked participants to keep a diary of what they did, classifying behaviours as either hedonic or eudaimonic. They found that those whose days were filled with more eudaimonic activity had greater meaning, positive feelings and satisfaction with life.[9]

These findings have led some to ask if increasing the level of eudaimonic activity in a person's life can be beneficial. In one such study, Veronika Huta and Richard Ryan randomly allocated participants into two groups. Those in the hedonic group were asked to add at least one more hedonic activity to their daily routine. These were activities like sleeping more, listening to music, watching TV and socialising more. Those in the eudaimonic group added at least one more eudaimonic activity. These were activities like helping someone else, studying more, having meaningful conversation with someone and counting one's blessings. Participants could choose their own activity. Over the ten days of the study, participants' activities were carefully monitored along with their well-being. What the researchers found was that increased hedonic orientation produced better well-being results at the end of the ten days, but when participants were contacted again three months later to see how well they were doing, the opposite was found: it was those in the eudaimonic group who showed better results in well-being.[10]

The long-term benefits of eudaimonia

The benefits of eudaimonia also seem to be long lasting and protective of mental-health difficulties. In a study that my colleague Alex Wood and I conducted, 5,603 people completed surveys to measure their eudaimonic well-being at two points in their lives: in their mid-fifties and in their mid-sixties. We found that those who scored lower on eudaimonic well-being in their mid-fifties were over seven times more likely to be depressed ten years later.[11]

Sadly, although it is a eudaimonic life that is better for us, consumer culture sells us a hedonistic lifestyle, involving greed, selfishness and exploitation. This by no means leads to greater well-being. Studies show that the more we focus on the pursuit of pleasure at the expense of developing and using the best of ourselves, the more we are likely to live a life bereft of meaning and success.

As we have seen, eudaimonia involves developing the best within ourselves. Indeed, as we saw earlier, the term eudaimonia means the 'true self'.

What is the flourishing life?

Authenticity is central to eudaimonia, as shown in the illustration opposite. Authenticity gives rise to a flourishing life and all that involves in terms of pursuing goals that are more intrinsically motivating to us and making the most of our talents and abilities. This in turn leads to a sense of meaning and purpose, and engaging more deeply in our work and leisure activities. As we flourish we are more able to achieve excellence

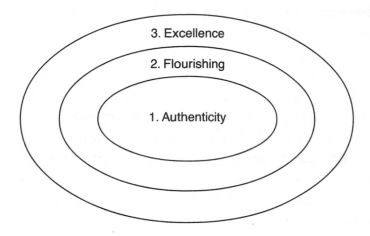

in what we do.

Authenticity is the core of human flourishing and excellence

Be intrinsically motivated

With authenticity, our personal growth is promoted, leading to a more flourishing life, because we are more in tune with ourselves and more able to set goals that allow us to live our lives in such a way as to be congruent with our intrinsic values and goals.

For the last two decades, Tim Kasser, one of the leading positive psychologists, and his colleagues have been studying people's values and goals. They have identified two types of goals and values. *Extrinsic* goals and values are those that people have when they 'buy into' the messages of consumer culture and organise their lives around the pursuit of money, possessions, image and status. The reason he refers to these as 'extrinsic' is because such pursuits are typically a means to some other end.

Advertisers use the idea of authenticity to sell us their products. From a well-known soft drink that purports to be the real thing to bottled sauces that promise us the genuine taste of Italy, we are sold the aspiration of living an authentic life. Of course, the reality is that the consumption of such products is often anything but authentic. We surround ourselves with the façade of authenticity while the very consumer culture that we have bought into pushes us further away from authenticity. We are sold a vision of the good life that tells us through powerful advertising campaigns that the good life is 'the goods life'. This is a phrase used by Kasser, who has argued that the message that happiness comes from the attainment of wealth and the purchase and acquisition of goods and services has become a pervasive factor of modern life. Consumer culture sells us a false bill of goods, Kasser says, that derails our ability to satisfy our basic psychological needs. It promotes hedonism at the expense of the eudaimonic life.

On the other hand, *intrinsic* goals and values involve striving for personal growth, intimacy and contribution to the community. Intrinsic goals and values are inherently more satisfying to pursue because they satisfy the deeper psychological needs that are necessary for happiness.[12]

Think about what drives you. Some people who go to work each day find their jobs interesting, meaningful and even enjoyable; others go to work solely because financial pressures demand it – they do not have any intrinsic interest in what they are doing. Ideally, as we strive towards authenticity, we seek a balance in our work between the extrinsic demands on us to earn our living and our intrinsic motivations to do what is meaningful to us. The authentic person seeks to prioritise their intrinsic motivations in order to find ways in which they can bring more of their talents and abilities to their work. It is not always easy and it may only be in small ways that they achieve this at first but, over time, and with effort, it may be possible to make a real difference.

Some are driven from an early age to prioritise their intrinsic motivations. As a university teacher, I see the differences between those who are intrinsically and extrinsically motivated every day. Some students are driven by their curiosity and an inner desire to learn and develop themselves personally. They may have ambitions to get high grades or build their careers, but that is not what drives them to their studies. For others, there is little interest in learning and challenging themselves; their aim is purely to obtain good grades and move on to the next stage of their career plan.

Prioritising well-being

Evidence from a number of studies shows that how people prioritise their goals and values is related to well-being. Generally speaking, the extent to which people prioritise intrinsic over extrinsic goals has been associated with higher self-reported levels of well-being. This is true across children, adolescents and adults, in a variety of cultures. And it is not just our own well-being we are talking about; those who prioritise intrinsic goals and values are also more likely to help others, try to understand other people's points of view, be more collaborative and less judgemental and are caring towards how we all live together on this same planet.

The values that are derived from intrinsic motives and goals are inherently healthy. Intrinsic motives express the basic psychological needs of the person that reflect their motivations towards psychological growth and self-actualisation. Satisfying these needs is therefore a key to well-being. In contrast, extrinsic motives derive from the need to obtain other people's approval, admiration and praise, and from the need to avoid social censure and punishment.[13]

Extrinsic values become a problem when they are more prominent in a person's life than intrinsic values, or when what Tim Kasser calls their 'relative intrinsic versus extrinsic value orientation' (RIEVO) is skewed towards extrinsic values. What's important is not so much what people say their values are but the extent to which they live them, by taking actions to do what they say is important. Research shows that well-being is more strongly related to doing the 'right' things than simply saying the right things are important.[14]

Authenticity is when we are able to tune out from the external messages telling us what should be important to us so that we can reprioritise our goals and values in a way that is consistent with our own inner voice, which will guide us towards intrinsic goals and values.

Identify your strengths

According to Seligman, we are using our character strengths when:

- What we are doing gives us a sense of being our real selves
- We feel we are learning
- We use existing skills in new ways
- It feels right to do what we are doing
- We feel invigorated
- We feel excitement and enthusiasm[15]

Christopher Peterson, along with Seligman, was one of the founders of positive psychology, and the co-developer of the *Classification of Strengths* project. The aim of their project was to devise a classification scheme to summarise the strengths of character that make the good life possible. Peterson and Seligman examined the notion of character strengths across cultures and history. They searched literature that discussed good character – from psychiatry, religion, philosophy and psychology – with the aim of identifying an exhaustive list of core character strengths. By that they meant personal traits that were ubiquitous across time and place, contributed to individual fulfilment, happiness and satisfaction, and were morally valued in their own right and not for the outcomes they led to.

They ended up with a list of 24 character strengths, organised into 6 broad categories:

Wisdom and knowledge These are strengths that include a love of learning, having a sense of perspective, being creative, curious and using critical thinking.

Courage These are strengths that involve our will to achieve goals in the face of challenges, such as when we are brave, we persevere and approach life with zest.

Love These are strengths that involve nurturing others, such as when we value close relationships, are kind to others and show empathy and social intelligence.

Justice These are strengths that underpin healthy community life such as teamwork, fairness and leadership.

Temperance These are strengths such as forgiveness, humility, prudence and self-control.

Transcendence These are strengths that create meaning in our lives such as being appreciative, playful, showing gratitude and being hopeful.[16]

Peterson and Seligman's work was revolutionary. It turned on its head psychology's preoccupation with character deficits and challenged psychologists to ask new questions about the causes and consequences of character *strengths*. We all have particular character strengths that most strongly define who we are. One person's strength might be curiosity, for example, while another person's is kindness or a love of learning. We all have our own strengths, but we don't always use them enough. We need to find ways to maximise the use of our strengths and cultivate the ones that are less strong. The more we seek to know ourselves, own ourselves and be ourselves, the more natural it will be for us to do this.

Seek meaning and purpose in life

Meaning means having a bigger picture about what your life is about. As you become more authentic and in touch with your inner voice of wisdom, you naturally begin to relate to yourself in ways that involve asking questions about what makes your life worthwhile and in what ways you make a difference.

Most of us inherit a set of meanings through exposure to what others tell us when we are young, be they customs, religious practices or whatever, and it takes time to work out for ourselves what really matters and what's important to us. Being open to the world around us and being mindful of what's inside us challenges old beliefs and values.

As we become more authentic, the sort of activities we engage in shift to those that are intrinsically interesting to us. Not only do we achieve a greater sense of meaning and purpose, but we also find more flow in our lives.

Become absorbed in activities to find 'flow'

The psychologist Mihalyi Csikszentmihalyi (pronounced 'chicks sent me high') identified the state we go into when we are absorbed in what we are doing as 'flow'.[17] Csikszentmihalyi was interested in how artists maintain their concentration for such long periods of time. What he discovered was how for the painters he studied it was doing the art itself that was so rewarding to them. Most of us will have had that same experience at some time or other where we are so immersed in what we are doing that time melts away. So absorbed are we in the task that we do not notice what else is going on around us. Colloquially, we might refer to it as 'being in the zone' and it can happen not only during artistic activities but also through sport, dancing, singing, sex, socialising, writing, gaming and, yes, even working. Perhaps the most important aspect of flow states is that we are engaged in activity for the sake of that activity, not for any rewards afterwards or because of external pressure to do so, but simply because we like doing it.

I mentioned that flow can take place even during working, and for many people this is true. They are lucky enough to have jobs that they love doing. But, sadly, for most of us this isn't the case. Or at least the opportunities for flow at work are slight. As such, it is common to seek flow experiences outside work as part of our leisure and even to think that work is meant to be lifeless. It shouldn't have to be and, in fact, wise employers know that if they want to get the best out of their employees, finding ways to make their work intrinsically enjoyable for its own sake is not only in the employees' best interest but also benefits the employer.

Authentic people are what Csikszentmihalyi refers to as 'autotelic', that is to say they have the curiosity, openness and drive to be motivated by intrinsic rewards.

Follow your passion

Authentic people follow their passion. As we have seen, when we are able to do what we love, we are more in tune with ourselves and our natural strengths and talents. Too often, we don't follow our passions in life, for the reasons we have discussed earlier, such as our conditions of worth. We get on with doing the things that our conditions of worth dictate that we do, and we put our passions to one side, perhaps thinking that sometime in the future we will get round to doing what we truly love. Authentic people dive right in.

Face reality

The inauthentic life can be a way of protecting us from the terrors of reality; for example, some scholars have pointed out how the materialistic values of Western society divert our attention away from the awful anxiety provoking truths of our lives; however, authentic people do not shy away from the realities of life. They are open to the hard truths:

- One day we will all die. That day might be today or tomorrow.
- We cannot control the world around us and we are helpless in the face of the unavoidable unpredictable things that will happen to us.
- We have to make decisions in life; we are responsible for the choices we make and we have to live with the consequences.
- There is no meaning or purpose to our lives except that which we choose to give it.
- Ultimately we are alone.

The authentic person lives life moment by moment, striving to understand themselves, their motivations, defences and conditions of worth, while being aware of their responsibilities and choices.

They look to their future goals, visualise their ideal future selves, imagine everything works out as they wish and think about the steps it would take to get there. They are mindful and deliberately look to ways to understand themselves and their experiences in new ways. They are compassionate towards themselves and others and will spend time thinking about their warm feelings towards others and to themselves. They are grateful and will spend time thinking of those to whom they feel grateful and will often say so in person. They are appreciative of life and will spend time counting their blessings. They will perform acts of kindness without any ulterior motives. Authenticity is the glue that binds together all of these things that people do, which they just do for no other reason. And when we do live authentically, we also benefit from achieving our greatest level of excellence in success in what we do, because we are at our best.

As we flourish as human beings, we are continually learning about ourselves and playing to our strengths, talents and abilities. Authentic people are always learning about themselves and realistically adjusting their self-image to navigate the world in ways that play to their strengths. Our lives become more meaningful and purposeful, our relationships improve, we have a sense of mastery over our environment and we continually seek out new opportunities for personal growth.

There are many things that make up a flourishing life, as we have seen: intrinsic aspirations, meaning and purpose, flow, and so on. But authenticity is the key that can unlock everything else. Right at the heart of positive change is the ability to know ourselves, own ourselves and be ourselves. All else follows.

The domino effect of authenticity

In summary, authenticity leads to a domino effect. As we become more authentic, one consequence leads to another in a chain reaction until our lives take on a new shape and direction that is more in tune with who we are, our values, beliefs, strengths, talents and abilities.

1 As we become more authentic, we become more open to experience and less defensive.
2 Consequently, we are more realistic about ourselves and the world around us.
3 That leads us to be more resilient and better at solving our problems.
4 As we solve our problems, our psychological adjustment improves.
5 As we become more psychologically adjusted, it becomes easier to be more authentic.
6 As we become even more authentic, we become better at accepting ourselves and, as a result, we see ourselves more realistically.
7 We become more mindful about the direction we are taking in life.
8 We become more creative and likely to engage in intrinsic activities that express who we are.
9 As we engage in activities that express who we are, we are more likely to make use of our strengths, find meaning and purpose and be in states of flow. In short, we flourish.
10 When we flourish, we value integrity, strive for excellence and achieve success in what we do.

I am convinced that the single most important key to a good life is to live it in a way that is absolutely true to oneself. In the next chapter, I will turn to the science of authenticity and some of the new research.

Chapter 7

The Authenticity Scale

Authenticity has been the topic of much theorising, as we have seen in the previous chapters, but research by positive psychologists is now producing scientific evidence of its influence on patterns of behaviour.[18] The Authenticity Scale was developed by myself and my colleagues Alex Wood, Alex Linley, John Maltby and Michael Baliousis, to assess the three components of knowing oneself, owning oneself and being oneself.[19]

EXERCISE: The Authenticity Scale

Rate each of the following twelve items from 1 (does not describe me at all) to 7 (describes me very well).

1   I think it is better to be yourself than to be popular   —
2   I don't know how I really feel inside   —
3   I am strongly influenced by the opinions of others   —
4   I usually do what other people tell me to do   —
5   I always feel I need to do what others expect me to do —
6   Other people influence me greatly   —
7   I feel as if I don't know myself very well   —

8   I always stand by what I believe in   —
9   I am true to myself in most situations   —
10   I feel out of touch with the 'real me'   —
11   I live according to my values and beliefs   —
12   I feel alienated from myself*   —

First, add up your answers to items 2, 7, 10 and 12. The main characteristic of authentic people is that they know themselves well. To achieve authenticity, people must be open to experience so that they are always learning about themselves, their strengths and weaknesses, and their likes and dislikes, and they must be open to new experiences. But most of us struggle to truly know ourselves. The opposite of knowing oneself is self-alienation. Few people ever know themselves so well that they are not to some degree alienated from themselves. If you scored above 12, you probably would like to know yourself more fully and often feel at least a niggling sense that life is not as it should be. Scores of 12 or under indicate that you probably feel you know yourself well.

Second, add up your answers to items 3, 4, 5 and 6. Owning ourselves means we are able to resist external pressures and take responsibility for our actions. Few of us are able to resist external pressures all of the time. For most of us, there will be times when we give in and say or do things at the request of others, even when we don't want to. If you scored above 12, you probably feel that you would like to be more able to resist external influences and stand your ground. Scores of 12 or under indicate that you probably feel a strong sense of self-ownership.

Third, add up your scores on items 1, 8, 9 and 11 to calculate how much you are able to be yourself. If you scored 20 or above, you are probably the sort of person who knows what he or she likes. You are prepared to stand your ground publicly when you need to, and you are able to be yourself in most situations. If you scored under 20, then it is likely that you would like to be more able to be yourself.

Whatever scores you achieved, they are not fixed in stone for ever, they simply describe how you generally are in your life right now. Authenticity is not like eye colour, which remains the same throughout our lives. It is a way of being ourselves that we learn – one that can become habitual, but ultimately we can change it if we so choose.

How you are day to day will also vary, so your scores on this questionnaire will not tell you precisely what you will do in any given situation; but it might give you a clue about what you are most likely to do.

Questionnaires such as the one above are often used in research to examine the differences between people scoring high and low on authenticity.[20] In research by Alison Lenton at the University of Edinburgh, it was found that people seem motivated to deliberately seek out experiences in which they feel authentic and to avoid situations in which they feel inauthentic, and that how likely they were to do this was, in part, determined by their scores on the Authenticity Scale.[21]

Of course, how a person behaves in any given situation will be influenced by a number of factors, particularly in social or work situations where there are other people present, but on the whole, research is showing us that there are some general patterns of behaviour associated with being authentic. It is to such research that we will now turn.

Authentic people are happier

Our research using the Authenticity Scale described above showed us that, on average, people who score higher on being themselves, owning themselves and knowing themselves are happier, more fulfilled and satisfied with life. This, and many other studies since, have shown that on average those who score higher on questionnaires assessing authenticity also score higher on questionnaires assessing happiness.[22]

People experience themselves as happier when they are most authentic. In the above-mentioned study by Alison Lenton, participants were asked to describe when they felt 'most me' or 'least me'. They were asked to say where they were, who was there and what they were doing. Most-me descriptions involved having fun, in a familiar place with familiar people doing familiar things, as well as achievement and success and being close with others. Least-me situations were those involving difficult events, feeling judged by others, awkward social interactions and trying something new. Not surprisingly, most-me situations involved positive emotions such as enjoyment, relaxation, excitement and love, whereas least-me situations involved anxiety, depression, anger and disappointment.[23] Authentic people, therefore, do seem to be happier. But a note of caution: such research does not tell us which comes first – happiness or authenticity. Correlation does not imply causality. Yet, if the theory of authenticity is correct as described in the previous chapter, we should find that authenticity leads to happiness. To confirm this, though, we need a completely different study in which people are followed over time in order to see whether authenticity at the earlier time point predicts well-being at the later time.

Researchers at Louisiana Tech University collected information from 232 college students on their authenticity, life satisfaction and levels of distress at two points in time separated by almost two months. They found that those who showed greater authenticity at the first time point were more satisfied with life and less distressed at the second time point,[24] so it does seem likely that authenticity leads to happiness.

Further support that authenticity leads to happiness comes from an ingenious study published by Yona Kifer and colleagues at Tel Aviv University.[25] In their study, participants were assigned randomly to one of two groups. Those in the first group were instructed to recall and write about a situation in which they were authentic:

> Please recall a particular incident in which you felt authentic. By authentic, we mean a situation in which you were true to yourself and experienced yourself as behaving in accordance with your true thoughts, beliefs, personality, or values. Try to relive this situation in your imagination. Please describe this situation in which you felt authentic – what happened, how you felt, etc.

In contrast, those in the second group were instructed to recall and write about a situation in which they were inauthentic:

> Please recall a particular incident in which you felt inauthentic. By inauthentic, we mean a situation in which you were not true to yourself and experienced yourself as not behaving in accordance with your true thoughts, beliefs, personality, or values. Try to relive this situation in your imagination. Please describe this situation in which you felt inauthentic – what happened, how you felt, etc.

Immediately after doing this, participants completed a test of happiness related specifically to how they were feeling at the present time. Remarkably, those in the first group who were simply asked to recall being authentic were happier than those in the second group who were asked to recall inauthenticity.

Try the above experiment for yourself by thinking about a situation in which you were true to yourself and experienced yourself as behaving in accordance with your true thoughts, beliefs, personality or values. Indeed, so effective can this be that I sometimes ask my clients to recall a time when they felt most authentic. Their answers can be revealing and can help them to begin to set new goals for themselves.

CASE STUDY: *Margaret*

Margaret, who was going through a difficult divorce, told me that she felt most authentic when horse riding as a child growing up in Devon. Although horse riding wasn't an option for her at the current time in her life, as she had a busy job in the City, we discussed what it was about this experience that she experienced as authentic. Several months later, inspired by our conversation, I saw her again and she told me that she had taken up flying lessons. The idea had never occurred to her before we had talked, but flying had given her a new passion that helped her to deal with a difficult period in her life and engage in new activities that spoke to her passions and gave her a sense of flow.

What a smile can tell us

Further proving that expressions of authenticity are beneficial to us in the longer run, LeeAnne Harker and Dacher Keltner, psychologists at the University of California at Berkeley, published a study in which they analysed 114 pictures from the 1958 and 1960 Mills College yearbooks. Mills College is a private school for women in Oakland, California. Yearbooks contain the photographs of all the graduating students of that year. All but three of the women in the photographs analysed were smiling. But not all the smiles were the same. An authentic smile is accompanied by tiny wrinkles at the corners of the eye. These laugh lines result from a muscle called the *orbicularis oculi*, which rings the eye and contracts when people produce genuine, but not polite, smiles. Such an authentic smile is called a Duchenne smile. Harker and Keltner rated each woman's smile in each of the 111 pictures on a ten-point scale reflecting its Duchenneness. What made this research so important was that the women in the pictures were participants in a long-term study. Harker and Keltner knew whether, decades after the photographs, the women were satisfied with their lives and happily married. That meant they could test whether the smiles of the women in that brief moment could tell us about how the women's lives had unfolded over the next 40 years. Astoundingly, they found that the Duchenneness of the smile predicted greater satisfaction with life and happier marriages decades later.

Authentic people are healthier

Other studies consistently report that, on average, people who score higher on tests for authenticity are more satisfied with life, have higher self-esteem, are less likely to be depressed and anxious, feel more alert and awake, and may even have fewer physical symptoms such as headaches, shortness of breath, and aches and pains.[26]

Jennifer Bryan and her colleagues at the University of Houston carried out a survey of over 500 students, asking them about how lonely they felt, their mood, physical symptoms and how much alcohol they typically drank. They found that those who felt more lonely were also more depressed and anxious, had more physical symptoms and more drink problems. That's probably not surprising, but they also found that if those who felt lonely also scored highly on authenticity, then the feelings of depression and anxiety, physical symptoms and drink problems were not as intense. It seems that authenticity acts to protect people against the adverse health effects of loneliness.[27]

It is likely that authenticity is helpful to people's health in a number of ways, but most notably if people are in tune with, and appreciative of, their internal states they are more likely to choose to live healthier lives, will recognise earlier the signs and symptoms of illness, seek medical advice, and be more alert to when they are engaging in self-destructive behaviours. Also, authenticity is likely to foster the essential psychological resources that give people perspective on any difficulties they do experience, and help them manage emotional and environmental challenges.[28]

Let's look at some of the ways in which authenticity helps people to become more resourceful.

Authentic people are more virtuous

I have already suggested that authenticity is what we desire in ourselves. Some researchers have looked at the consequences of inauthenticity for how we feel about ourselves. Research suggests that authenticity leads people to feel morally virtuous. Francesca Gino and colleagues asked some participants to recall a time in their personal or professional life when they felt true to themselves. They then asked them to write for five to ten minutes about what it was like and their thoughts and feelings in the situation. Other participants were asked to recall an event in which they were untrue to themselves. It was found that inauthentic experiences led people to feel more impure and less moral. In a further study, after participants thought about events in which they were true or untrue to themselves, they were asked to complete words with letters missing, such as W_ _ H, SH _ _ ER and S _ _ P. These words could be completed as cleaning words (wash, shower, soap) or as neutral words (such as wish, shaker and step).

Participants who recalled an inauthentic experience generated more cleaning-related completions. In an ingenious final study, they again asked people to recall times when they had been true or untrue to themselves. Then, as part of the procedure, participants were given the chance to actually wash their hands. Finally, they were told they could make a donation to charity. What happened was that those in the inauthentic condition were more likely to donate to charity and the amount donated was greater in those who did not wash their hands. What this research tells us is how we feel moved within ourselves to be authentic and that when we engage in behaviours that don't feel true to ourselves we experience a need to cleanse ourselves in some way.[29] It seems that we are driven by the desire for authenticity and when we feel inauthentic we are motivated to take actions that increase our feelings of authenticity.

Authentic people are more realistic

Theory has it that authentic people are always learning about themselves and realistically adjusting their self-image to navigate the world in ways that play to their strengths. By definition, authentic people are less defensive and more open to experience – the central element of the eudaimonic life, as we saw in the previous chapter.

In everyday life we are confronted with situations that threaten our self-image, such as when we fail at a task at work or say something inappropriate to someone we love and cause an argument. The truth is that we often find some way of not taking responsibility for our mistakes – we blame others, refuse to admit our failings, and so on. We use our psychological defences to stop ourselves hearing the truth. We do not want to hear that we are not as clever, witty, attractive or liked as we tell ourselves. If you think this doesn't apply to you, reflect on the fact that when studies have asked people to rate their intelligence, sense of humour or attractiveness, most people rate themselves as above average. Of course, it can't be true that most people are above average, so the conclusion is that a lot of people lack insight into themselves.

Few of us have a completely realistic self-image. We hide from knowing ourselves because the pain of self-knowledge can seem too great. Sometimes a little positive self-deception is helpful, but when our style of coping is overwhelmingly defensive, the chances are we are in poor mental health – something our friends and colleagues are sure to recognise even if we don't.

Strategies we resort to when we fear failure

One way we protect ourselves from threatening self-knowledge is through self-handicapping. Self-handicapping is when people fear failure and are uncertain of their ability to succeed at a task: for example, just before an important singing audition we might claim we are ill. We might even convince ourselves that this is the case. We go into the audition and apologise for our sore throat before we sing the first notes. Self-handicapping is a topic studied by social psychologists interested in how people create and find impediments that reduce the likelihood of good performance or that act as 'insurance' against the possibility that it might not be a good performance. Both are means of protecting our self-esteem. If we fail, then we can attribute our failure to something beyond our control.

People self-handicap in two ways. Behavioural self-handicapping is when we do things ourselves, such as drink too much alcohol, don't put enough music practice in, or spend our time doing something other than what we need to do. Self-reported handicapping is when we report feeling ill or suffering from anxiety, or other psychological problems. Both of these operate in different ways. Behavioural self-handicapping does actually reduce our chances of success, whereas self-reported handicapping simply saves face if we fail, but, by itself, it doesn't reduce our chances of success. In general, although self-handicapping can protect our self-esteem, it is not what mentally healthy people do, and the self-esteem that it protects is built on self-deception.

In a fascinating study, Ahmet Akin and Ümran Akin at Sakarya University in Turkey[30] asked students to complete a Turkish version of the Authenticity Scale and the Self-handicapping Scale, which consists of 25 statements that people agree or disagree with. An example is, 'I try not to get too intensely involved in competitive activities, so that it won't hurt too much if I lose or do poorly.' They found that those who scored higher on the Self-handicapping Scale were less likely to know themselves, own themselves and be themselves. Authentic people, it would seem, have less need for such defensive strategies as self-handicapping, because they do not worry about protecting their self-image.

Authenticity – the mindful approach

In contrast, authentic people cherish learning about themselves. They do not deny or distort information that challenges their perceptions of themselves but approach new situations with an open mind, accepting both the positive and negative aspects.

In a related study to test for defensiveness, Chad Lakey and colleagues interviewed people using a special set of questions. The first five questions are straightforward and designed to ease people into the interview. The final five questions are designed to put them at ease after the interview by asking them about their most enjoyable experiences. But the 15 questions in the middle are designed to put them under the spotlight. These ask about challenging times in their life – such as when they have done something unethical or felt sexually undesirable. People react in a variety of ways to these awkward questions, ranging from being verbally defensive to answering the question clearly and directly. As expected, those who are skilled at unbiased processing are less defensive. According to their explanation, authentic people are more mindful. Authentic people, they showed in further studies, are more able to focus their attention and awareness on immediately present stimuli in a non-judgemental manner.[31]

Authentic people play to their strengths

Not surprisingly, authentic people spend more time doing the things they truly love – the activities that they are passionate about and make them feel alive. Being less defensive and more open to experience, they are inclined to develop their enduring strengths, interests and inclinations that predispose them to benefit from some activities more than others.

As we saw earlier, Christopher Peterson and Martin Seligman surveyed tens of thousands of people of all ages in different countries, finding that the more people are able to use their character strengths in their daily lives, the happier and healthier they are. In one study, for example, people were asked to think of what they would ideally consider to be their most fulfilling job, their truest love, their best friend and their most engaging hobby. In answering these questions, people did not always describe their current jobs, relationships or leisure activities and the things that people commonly strive for in life such as status, salary, good looks or pleasure. Rather, what they described were jobs, relationships and leisure pursuits consistent with their character strengths; for example, people whose character strength was a love of learning would happily be found reading in their spare time. Those whose strength was kindness said that they would enjoy jobs that involved helping others. And people who were particularly curious would hanker after relationships with adventurous types.

Authentic people have more meaning in their lives

If authentic people are more likely to use their character strengths, it's not surprising that when people strive for authentic lives they also find themselves living more meaningful lives. This finding was demonstrated by Rebecca Schlegel and her colleagues at the University of Missouri in an ingenious set of studies. In one study, participants were invited to the laboratory to take part in an experiment. The first task they were given was to circle 10 words from a list of 60 descriptive words (such as 'warm', 'friendly' and 'outgoing') that described their true self, defined as, 'Those characteristics that you possess and would like to express socially, but are not always able to, for whatever reason. Think of only those traits that you are able to express around those people you are closest to.' Participants also completed a questionnaire designed to score how much meaning they had in their life. Finally, participants were given a computer task. Words from the original descriptive list were presented on the screen and participants were asked to respond as quickly as possible to each word by pressing a button labelled 'Me' or another labelled 'Not Me'. The researchers found that those who were fastest at correctly identifying 'Me' scored highest on meaning in life. The reason, the researchers argued, is that authenticity is the hub of meaning, so those who know themselves better are able to interpret life experiences in a more meaningful way.[32]

*

Perhaps related to this is the observation that authentic people seem to have a clearer direction in life. A study of students by Nathan White and Terence Tracey at Arizona State University found that those who scored higher on authenticity were less indecisive about their careers.[33] And those who found themselves trapped in jobs that they find dissatisfying and meaningless might feel compelled to find a new and more meaningful direction. Sara Hirschorn and Kate Hefferon at the University of East London interviewed ten people in their late twenties and thirties who had left their careers to go travelling around the world. Their participants described how they had to face the fear that came with making such a big decision but that once they had made the leap there was a sense of being more alive and true to themselves.[34]

Authentic people are grittier

Grit refers to a person's drive to succeed. It involves having passion and the perseverance to overcome setbacks along the way in order to achieve your goals. Mia Vainio and Daiva Daukantaitė at Lund University in Sweden carried out two surveys, the first with students and the second with older, working adults. In both surveys, participants completed questionnaires to assess their levels of authenticity and their grit. The researchers found that those who scored higher on authenticity were also more likely to score higher on a measure of grit. Authentic people will be more motivated to pursue their goals no matter what it takes.[35] Not surprisingly, authentic people seem also to cope better with stress.

Authentic people cope better with stress

There are different ways of coping with stress. Psychologists have identified three broad ways of coping that they have labelled problem-focused coping, emotion-focused coping and avoidant coping.

Problem-focused coping involves attempts to resolve difficulties by taking steps to remove threats and find solutions. Those who use problem-focused coping are able to narrow their attention to the problems at hand and not let other competing activities get in their way. If they need to, they get help from others. They don't get distracted from what they need to do.

Emotion-focused coping involves managing one's emotions. When we are upset we need to be able to do this. Commonly we may seek sympathy from friends and talk about how we are feeling.

Avoidance coping is when we try not to think about the situation or we find ways to shut out our feelings. Turning to alcohol is, of course, one way, but people find all sorts of ways to disengage from their feelings or distract themselves from what needs to be done.

As we have seen, authentic people are more in touch with reality, and so it is not surprising to find that, compared to less authentic people, those high on authenticity tend to be more problem- and emotion-focused but less avoidant. Authentic people take the bull by the horns when they need to.[36] Most notably, authentic people are more active in their coping, concentrating their efforts on removing threats and reducing the impact of threat to themselves and they are less likely to turn to substance use as way of dealing with their problems.

Another way in which authenticity improves people's lives is through the quality of their relationships.

Authentic people live more harmoniously with others

It is only when people are alienated from themselves that they act in destructive ways. Putting evidence behind the theory, Diana Pinto at the University of Leicester devised a study to test how people high in authenticity behave in social situations compared to people low in authenticity. She asked participants to engage in a computer task in the laboratory. All they had to do was press a button in relation to a message that appeared on the screen. If they pressed a certain button in the time allocated, they earned points that they could exchange for money. The twist was that they were told that they were playing against another person in an adjoining laboratory who could steal points from them. The task was designed to mirror real-life situations where people might sometimes take credit for others' hard work.

The experiment was, in fact, rigged so that participants were not actually playing against another person – the idea being that by thinking that someone else was stealing points from them, the participants would feel cheated and be provoked to play the game aggressively. To test for aggression, they were told that they could steal points from their opponent next door if they wished.

What the researchers found was that players who scored high on authenticity were actually less likely to respond aggressively. They continued to do their best to earn points for themselves rather than turning their attention to getting their own back – they were less punitive towards others. It was people who scored low on authenticity who were more likely to behave aggressively despite this being at some personal cost – by behaving aggressively, participants lost even more of their own points.[37]

Authentic people have deeper relationships

Over my coffee one morning I read the lonely hearts in the newspaper. Out of the 89 women seeking men, 21 per cent described
themselves as sincere, genuine or honest and 14 per cent were
looking for such qualities in their potential partners. The figures
were similar for men seeking women. We desire authenticity in
our friends, family and colleagues and we know that this is what
others want in us too.[38] I'm not sure, however, that it is worth
mentioning in a lonely hearts advert, as most people think of
themselves as authentic and, of course, as we have seen, one of
the problems is that we don't always know ourselves well enough
to realise that we lack authenticity.

My advice to anyone writing a lonely heart advert is to ask
for observable behavioural qualities, such as liking walking,
watching films, enjoying wine or days out at museums. At least
that way you can quickly ascertain if they have expertise, knowledge of such things, or at least a genuine interest. At the same
time, you can gauge their authenticity when you meet them. In
relationships, we are deeply attentive to whether our partners
are authentic, and it is authenticity that is the glue that holds
relationships together.

There is an important caveat, however. For a relationship to
last, you have to be able to be yourself, but being yourself isn't
necessarily desirable when you are first setting off on a romantic
relationship.

William Swann and colleagues at the University of Texas
surveyed 176 married and dating couples.[39] Partners in each
couple were sat at opposite ends of a table and asked to complete a questionnaire describing first themselves and then their
partners. The table was long enough so that they could not see
each other's answers. Married people were most intimate with
spouses whose evaluations mirrored their own self-ratings;
dating people were most intimate with partners who evaluated

them favourably. At the start of a relationship we evaluate the other person as a potential long-term partner and mate, and we don't necessarily want others to see the real us, but as the relationship deepens we do. In fact, the researchers found that married people wanted to be known for who they are, regardless of whether they think highly of themselves; it wasn't just those with a positive self-image who wanted to be seen for themselves – everyone did.

CASE STUDY: *Joe*

The message is that in long-term relationships we need to feel accepted for who we are, otherwise we will withdraw from the relationship. This is what happened to Joe. In his forties and recently divorced from his wife, Joe couldn't believe his luck when he met Patricia. She was attractive and intelligent, and Joe was absolutely besotted by her. There was no doubt in his mind that this was the woman he had been waiting all his life to meet. He put his all into the relationship and, right from the beginning, made his feelings clear to Patricia. At first he didn't notice that she had most of the power in the relationship. She was more uncertain about the relationship and, whereas Joe was eager for them to set up home together and begin their new life, Patricia put the brakes on by asking Joe to slow down. It was clear that Joe was more enthusiastic than Patricia and so the balance of power was in Patricia's favour.

After a few months, Joe did notice, because he realised that he was always the one to pay for meals out in the evening, trips to the theatre and so on, but he didn't care, because he was still so much in love. But then, after some more months, Joe realised that even though they had now been together for nearly a year he didn't feel able to be himself with Patricia. 'I realised that she didn't really know me. I was still putting on an act to impress her and to win her. I was always on my best behaviour and still scared that if she saw the real me I wouldn't be enough for her.' What Joe experienced was how an imbalance of power in a relationship can lead to inauthenticity.

Joe was also pinning his view of himself on the ups and downs of the relationship. When all was going well, he thought well of himself, but when it was going badly he thought less of himself.

When people's self-worth is tied to the fluctuations in their relationship, psychologists call this relationship-contingent self-esteem.[40]

Some people can also lose the sense of who they are in a relationship, in a way that reminds me of the mating life of the anglerfish. When the male of the species reaches maturity, its digestive system shuts down and it is unable to feed. The male is programmed by evolution to seek out a female. Females are about 40 times bigger than the males. The male latches on to a female and releases an enzyme that permanently attaches him to her. The male is now completely dependent on the female for nutrients. The two organisms merge. Eventually, the male disintegrates and all that is left is a lump on the side of the female. In a metaphorical sense, sometimes people form relationships in which one person disappears into the personality of the other.

Testing for the balance of power in a relationship

Kristin Neff and Marie-Anne Suizzo, two psychologists at the University of Texas, investigated this issue in a study in which they asked people to rate who has the most say in their relation-ship – them or their partner.[41] You are shown a five-point visual scale like the one below:

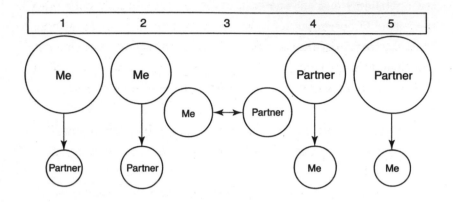

Rate the balance of power in your relationship

You are asked to think about your relationship. If you think you have by far the most power, then you would choose image 1, which represents you in the most dominant position (as the bigger circle). The next image is also you in a dominant position, but not quite as dominant as in 1. The middle image represents equality. Conversely, if you think your partner has the most power, then you would choose either images 4 or 5, which represent you in subordinate positions (as the smaller circle). Neff and Suizzo found that those who perceived themselves to be in subordinate relationships were more likely to admit that they acted in a false way with their partner and felt less able to be themselves with their partner.

For long-term relationships to flourish, authenticity is vital. Frederick Lopez at the University of Houston and Kenneth Rice at the University of Florida identified two key components: unac-ceptability of deception and intimate risk-taking.[42]

Unacceptability of deception refers to when people feel it to be important to be themselves in their relationship, even if it means their partner doesn't always see them at their best. Such people desire to be truly known by their partner for who they are, their strengths and weaknesses, and to know their partner for who they are. They prefer to have open and frank conversations. They desire truthfulness in their relationship, even if at times it can reveal things that are disappointing. Think about your own attitude to deception by reading the statements below:

- To avoid conflict in our relationship, I will sometimes tell my partner what I think he or she wants to hear, even if it's not true.
- I purposefully hide my true feelings about some things in order to avoid upsetting my partner.

If you disagree with these two statements then you are probably someone who has a high degree of unacceptability of deception.

Intimate risk-taking refers to when people desire to share their deepest thoughts and feelings with their partner. They don't want there to be secrets in their relationship, even if sometimes that may lead to disagreements. Their aim is to be completely themselves. Think about your own attitude to intimate risk-taking by reading the statements below:

- I feel free to reveal the most intimate parts of myself to my partner.
- There are no topics that are 'off limits' between my partner and me.

If you agree with these statements then you are probably someone who has a high degree of intimate risk-taking.

In their study, Lopez and Rice found that those who think it is unacceptable to deceive in a relationship and who favour intimate risk-taking are those who are most satisfied with their relationship. If we begin to become more authentic in our relationships, then there are two possible outcomes: the relationship might implode if the other person can't accept a more equal balance of power; or we will achieve the more desired equal balance of power. What is certain is that the relationship will not stay the same if we begin to avoid deception and favour intimate risk-taking.

We can think in a similar way about our power in other relationships in our lives, such as with friends, family and work colleagues. We might feel generally powerful in many areas of our life; or we may feel less powerful in some relationships than in others. Inevitably, such considerations will influence our expressions of authenticity. It is where we have low personal power that we are likely to feel the most inauthentic.

In relationships, allow authenticity to develop

Authenticity is the key to relationships, but at the same time this does not mean that we need to be completely open and transparent on a first meeting. As we have seen, it makes sense to reveal ourselves over time in an intricate dance of self-disclosure with another person. To show too much too soon of yourself can sabotage your attempts to get to know someone. I'm not saying don't be authentic on a first date, rather that you don't need to tell the person about your deepest fears and childhood traumas there and then. Too much self-revelation too soon will scare many people off. That does not mean being inauthentic, but rather going with the rhythm of the relationship that develops.

Authenticity means that you can be in a relationship on equal terms with another person; you do not look for, or instigate, some sort of power imbalance out of habits learned in your childhood about how people ought to be. You can also be open, honest and transparent in the relationship and appreciate the emotional and sexual intimacy for what it is in the moment. In these ways you are accepting of yourself as you are in the relationship.

Now that we have examined the idea of authenticity, and the research into why it matters, the next chapters will look at how you can begin to cultivate authenticity in your own life.

PART III

Three Steps Towards Authenticity: 30 Practical Exercises to Try

I must be willing to give up what I am in order to become what I will be.

Albert Einstein[1]

The following chapters are designed to offer you guidance in how to develop and deepen your own self-knowledge, ownership of yourself and ability to live authentically. Attempting to live an authentic life does not imply that you will never experience upsets or difficulties. What it does mean is that as you endeavour to approach your life, moment by moment, with the intention of being authentic, your life will take on a new shape and direction. Like tilting the rudder of a boat gently, you will be setting a new course. The authentic life is not a destination that you reach, but it is the journey that you are on.

Most people spend their lives in an agonising and defensive struggle to preserve their self-image. But, as the quote above suggests, the journey towards authenticity is different. You will need to dismantle what you think you are so that you can rebuild yourself anew.

In the following chapters I will explore these key messages and, along the way, offer some exercises and guidance that might be useful.

I will ask you to think about when and where and with whom you feel you can truly be yourself. You may behave differently in different situations. In some situations you might be more likely to stand your ground and argue for your point of view; in others you might back off, deciding it better to hold your tongue. You might be open when you are at home with your partner and say what you think, but when you arrive at work the next morning you know it is better to not say what you think, or vice versa. In reading the previous chapters you may already have begun to identify those situations when you can feel most or least true to yourself.

Part of the process of change might be that you wish to change the world around you in such a way that you begin to remove the blocks to authenticity in your life. You might also spend more time doing things – and with people and in places – that nurture your authenticity. I imagine that right now you might even be thinking about what blocks you need to remove and what activities you need to increase. Some of these may take time to engineer into your life, others might be things that you could do right now. That might send a chill up your spine as you imagine how difficult it might be to make some of those changes.

Becoming more of who you can be means that you may have to confront things that you have been fearful of facing up to in the past. You may begin to seem like a different person to those around you in ways that they find upsetting. In addition, you need to be willing to give up aspects of what you are right now to become what you can be. Embarking on a more authentic life requires you to be courageous and to be prepared to take the consequences of your actions.

You might be tempted to rush into new situations, but my advice would be to work through the book, think deeply about the exercises, take them step by step and realise that authenticity is a moment-by-moment journey not a final destination. You might also find that working through some of the exercises that follow are upsetting.

You might also realise that you have made inauthentic choices throughout your life that have led you to this point. You may now want to change this situation and you might even fantasise about going back to an earlier time and making those same choices again. Looking back at the crossroads of your life you would choose to pursue a different relationship, take a different course than the one you did, enter a different career, or whatever. Such thoughts can be overwhelming, and you may feel helpless and full of despair at the choices of your younger self.

The fact is, of course, that you can't go back, but you can start today to make each and every decision an authentic one from your heart. If that is your decision, the journey ahead will not always be easy but, in the future, you will not experience the regret that you do now if all your next decisions are authentic. You can't change your world overnight but you can take each step forward mindfully and purposefully. Finally, don't expect this to be easy. If you genuinely want to make changes in your life you will need to work hard, revisit the exercises in this book time and again and recognise that it might take some time before you begin to see big changes starting to happen. In the short term, however, you will gain confidence in yourself that you can change.

Step 1 – know yourself Step 1 refers to the process of looking deeply within yourself, to uncover your barriers to authenticity and to begin to dismantle them.

Step 2 – own yourself Approach your life with a sense of responsibility for your thoughts, emotions and actions, and the directions you are taking in life.

Step 3 – be yourself Step 3 encourages you to begin to put your new learnings into action and to practise new ways of being in the world.

You are now able to see what is ahead. Next, I will discuss each of the steps in detail and show you how to put into practice the lessons you have learned so far in this book. You may find it helpful to have a notebook to write down your thoughts as you go through the following exercises. It is of no matter if the answers to the exercises seem obvious, give it a go anyway, as you don't know what further insights deeper exploration will bring.

Chapter 8

Step 1 – Know Yourself

The following exercises are included to help you get to know yourself a bit better. Starting with an exercise on your personal history, we will work through other exercises related to how well you are aware of your strengths, values, fears and aspirations; what aspects of yourself you would like to change; whether your relationships nurture you; and, finally, your goals and authentic direction in life.

EXERCISE 1: Understand your personal history

The following list of questions is designed to get you thinking. Take your time over them. My suggestion is to set at least 20 minutes aside for this exercise. In your notebook, just write continuously for those 20 minutes. Let your thoughts flow freely and simply write whatever comes to mind, even if it seems ridiculous.

1 What does your name mean? For instance, was your name chosen for you to remember a particular relative? Does your name have significance for you and your family? Would you like to change your name? If so, why?

2 Do you have a nickname? What do you think it says
   about you? If you were to choose a nickname for
   yourself, what would it be?
3 What were your parents like? In what ways are you
   similar and how do you differ from them?
4 What did you most love doing as a child?
5 What books, films or music do you most like? What is it
   you like about these?
6 What is it you most like about yourself? Why?
7 What would you like to change about yourself?
8 How do you act when you feel frightened?

Come back to your answers later and spend another ten minutes
thinking about what you have written. When you come back to
your first answers, dig deeper. Keep asking yourself, 'What is my
reason for saying that?', 'What does my answer say about me?' If
you are reading this book with someone else, think about sharing
your answers.

EXERCISE 2: Unravel your blueprint

1 What are your first memories as a child when you
   remember yourself feeling joy? What were you doing?
   Take ten minutes and write in your journal, without
   stopping to think too much, about a time when as a
   child you remember doing something that felt joyful.
   The chances are you were using one of your natural
   strengths, talents or abilities to its full extent. There
   would have been sheer pleasure in the doing.
2 Now think about another time when you were miserable.
   Take ten minutes and write in your journal, without
   stopping to think too much, about a time when as a child
   you remember doing something that felt miserable. The

chances are that you were doing something at someone else's request that required you to use strengths, abilities or talents that you did not possess as much as when you were doing something joyful.

Left to our own devices, as children we will do the things that come naturally to us. We will use our strengths, interests and abilities. Through their use we will nurture them and develop them further. It is in this way that we grow into becoming ourselves. Looking back on our lives in this way can give us insight into what our natural strengths, interests and abilities are.

EXERCISE 3: Think of the people you most admire

These are not necessarily the people you like the most or who you are friends with, but the people whom you respect the most. They may be people you know or people in the public eye, or even people from history. Take five minutes to think of three people you admire. When you have done that, list what it is about these people that you most admire.

This exercise will give you insight into some of the qualities you would like to see more of in yourself.

EXERCISE 4: What are your values?

What is it you most value in life? Take five minutes to think what you would do if money or time were not an issue. What would you do in such an ideal situation? Your first response might be to say something like take a holiday or resign from your job, but what would you do after that? What are the things you would really want to spend your life doing, if you could? What does your answer tell you about your values and deep-seated motivations?

If money was not an issue, you might also want to give away a substantial sum to charity. Imagine you can only give to one charity. What sort of charity would it be? What is the cause you would most like to support? Why?

This exercise will give you insight into your values and what is most important to you.

EXERCISE 5: Let your unconscious give you clues

Look around the room you are in now and, without thinking about why, just pick an object that stands out for you. Don't think about it, but just quickly describe the object and use the word 'I' instead of 'it': for example, a woman who identified a single tattered glove said, 'I am old and half of me is missing.' A man who pointed out a lampstand said, 'I sit here on this shelf by myself day after day and only occasionally does someone turn me on so I can light up.' Both quickly realised that this was how they also felt about themselves.

Take some time to reflect on your own statements and what truth they have for you. Use it as a tool to learn about yourself.

EXERCISE 6: Pay attention to your dreams

1 Each morning as you wake, stay for a time in that half-awake state where you can recall your dream. Lie still and, keeping your eyes closed, try to recall each and every aspect of the dream.
2 When you have done that, take the pen and notebook

that you keep close by the bed to write down as much as you remember.

3 Each day that you do this, come back to what you have written later when you have time and go over your notes. Let ideas, thoughts and associations come to mind.

4 Do this regularly every few days for several weeks. You might have to set the alarm clock a little earlier to make space in your day for this, but you may be surprised at what you learn.

Many people dismiss their dreams and, even if they do remember some aspects when they wake in the morning, these are very quickly forgotten. In my view, this is a lost opportunity, as by paying attention to our dreams we can often learn valuable things about ourselves; however, it takes some practice.

EXERCISE 7: Identify in which of your relationships you are most authentic

Think about how authentic you are in your different relationships, such as that of mother, father, wife, husband, a role at work or with a group of friends. Choose three important relationships in your life and then ask yourself if you agree with each of the following statements for each of those relationships:

1 I experience being in this relationship as meaningful and valuable to me.

2 I have freely chosen to be in this relationship.

3 I can be myself in this relationship.

4 I feel valued in this relationship.

Did you agree with each of the statements for all three relationships? If not, you may need to face up to the reality that some of your relationships may be toxic to you and not allowing you to get the balance right where you have supportive relationships that allow you to be yourself.

By asking yourself these questions, you may now have insights into which of your relationships might be deserving of more of your time and energy.

EXERCISE 8: **When are you most you?**

To help people think about how on track they are with their lives, when I conduct workshops on authenticity, I sometimes start by asking participants to take a few minutes to think about the times that they have felt that they are being most true to themselves. Below are some examples of the answers that I have been given to this question:

- 'When I'm sitting at the river fishing, I just feel content and at one with the world.'
- 'When I'm setting out on a long walk on an autumn day knowing that the day is completely mine.'
- 'When I'm in the middle of a painting, I just lose myself in what I'm doing.'
- 'When I'm with the family and we have the whole weekend ahead of us.'
- 'I'm about to land a new contract and bring the vision I've had for years to reality.'

I also ask them to think about the times that they feel that they cannot be real. Below are some examples of the answers that people have given to this question:

- 'When I wake on a Monday morning and know that I've got to catch the train.'

- 'When I'm sitting in a meeting at work and I'm thinking: *What am I doing with my life?*'
- 'When the customer is unpleasant, but I'm smiling and being nice because I have to.'
- 'When I'm with my partner and I always seem to do what she wants and we never do things that interest me.'

Now think about the times you can be the *most you* and when you can be the *least you*.

1 When was the last time you felt that you were truly being yourself? Where were you? What were you doing? Who were you with? Come up with a list of three examples. Write down your answers to these questions in your notebook. Don't spend too much time thinking. Just start writing and the words will flow.

2 When was the last time you felt you were not being yourself? Where were you? What were you doing? Who were you with? Come up with a list of three examples.

3 Now think about what you would like to do less of and what you would like to do more of.

Your answers to these questions will provide you with a direction of travel towards a more authentic life and your ideal self.

EXERCISE 9: Visualise your ideal self

Let's start by thinking about your actual self and your ideal self. Your actual self is who you are right now. Your ideal self is who you would like to be.

1 To help you do this, first make a list of your weaknesses, as you see them. Try to come up with at least three statements; for example:

- I am three pounds overweight.
- I drink too many glasses of wine.
- I am not good at making friends.

2 Now rewrite your statements as discrepancies between your actual self and your ideal self; for example:

- My ideal self is three pounds lighter.
- My ideal self has only a glass of wine at the weekend.
- My ideal self is sociable and outgoing.

EXERCISE 10: Use the miracle question

1 Imagine you go to sleep tonight and you wake tomorrow morning. During the night a miracle happened and, when you wake up, your most positive dreams for your future have come true. Remember, a miracle has occurred, so you are waking up to your life as you would ideally like it to be. At this point, you may have only quite hazy visions of your ideal future, so to help you be specific about what the real world changes would be for you, think about your answers to the following questions:

A How do you feel when you wake?
B What is the first thing you will do?
C Your best friend arrives. Immediately, they notice that things have improved. What is it that they will have noticed?
D What happens next in your day?

2 Give a blow-by-blow account of the whole day of your ideal life when everything is just as you would ideally want it to be.
3 Would that be a typical day?
4 What would you be doing on the same day a week later?

This exercise is called the miracle question. It is a question that coaches often ask their clients[2] in order to help them think about what they want to change about themselves. Your answers to the questions will have helped you begin to think about this, but even so the questions are not always easy to answer. Often, people will immediately talk about having more money, a larger and more luxurious home, but when pushed to say more they may struggle to know how they would actually spend their time. Forced by the questions to go deeper within themselves, they begin to sharpen their focus for what their ideal life would be like.

It is worth coming back to the miracle question every so often, to dig even deeper into understanding what you would like to change.

———————

As you have worked through the above exercises, you probably had some thoughts that have surprised you.

Our degree of authenticity is shaped in childhood and learned through our life experiences, so it is changeable. Given the motivation to change, we can quite drastically reshape ourselves to become more authentic. However, for most people, this process is not a quick fix but a transition that takes weeks, months and even years. Getting to truly know ourselves is a lifelong process. Even if we already know ourselves to a great degree, there is always more to learn.

In the next chapter we will turn to the issue of owning yourself.

Chapter 9

Step 2 – Own Yourself

Authenticity demands that we face up to ourselves and tell the truth to ourselves. That is easier said than done, and it takes commitment to develop self-knowledge as well as perseverance in asking ourselves tough questions. This chapter is about how we take responsibility for ourselves and our choices in life, our ability to overcome our tendencies towards becoming defensive when we feel threatened, and how to move forward with full awareness of the consequences of our actions.

EXERCISE 1: Admit that you have made mistakes in the past and look to the future

1 Think about a mistake you have made that still troubles you. What can you learn about that experience? Take ten minutes to write down three things that you have learned.

2 Think about how you can put that learning into action in the future. Promise yourself that in the future you will use your mistakes as opportunities to learn about yourself.

Everyone makes mistakes, but some people get trapped in ruminating about the past and what they could have done differently. Such thoughts can become all-consuming and create misery for yourself and those around you. Part of the problem, however, is that too often we don't like to admit to ourselves that we have made mistakes or that we are at fault in any way. We do our best to maintain an image of ourselves as worthwhile, because the thought of having been in error challenges our view of ourselves as worthwhile human beings. Such thinking traps us in the past by fostering a rigid and out-of-date view of ourselves.

To move forward, we need to accept our past decisions and allow ourselves to learn about ourselves by being open to the causes of our setbacks, especially when it involves facing up to our responsibilities and taking ownership of our mistakes. By doing so, we become flexible in looking to the future and allowing ourselves to accommodate new experiences.

EXERCISE 2: Understand your defences

A way to begin to uncover your defences is to think back to an event that you feel ashamed of or guilty about. Take a few seconds to recall the event. Notice, first of all, that you don't feel like doing this and you might even be thinking about skipping this exercise. Even when you have brought the event to mind it might be hard to picture all the details. Keep thinking about the event and your reactions to it and notice how hard this is and the ways in which you keep trying to divert your attention.

To be able to live authentically you need to understand and combat your own tendencies towards using defences when situations are challenging. The point is to know when you are

lying to yourself. The truth is that a lot of the time the things
we tell ourselves are simply nonsense. 'I did everything I
could to help', 'It wasn't my fault', 'I was too busy, otherwise I
would have.' A lot of the time we may kid ourselves about our
motivations, feelings, responsibilities and desires.

EXERCISE 3: Use the five whys

1 Think of something that hasn't gone well for you in the
   last month. Perhaps it was a job interview, a meeting
   with a client or an argument with a partner. What was
   the reason?
2 Now, ask yourself the same question again and come up
   with a different answer. What other reasons?
3 Ask yourself again. What other reasons? Keep going
   until you have pushed yourself to give five or more
   reasons. By the fifth reason you should know if you
   have got a satisfactory reason that has pushed you to
   challenge yourself. If not, keep going.

This is a problem-solving technique originally developed by
Sakichi Toyoda in the 1970s for checking that car engines work
properly, but it works with our mental life equally well. It can
be quite a painful self-examination. Often the first response
that comes to mind is defensive. But at each next step you find
yourself going deeper into your understanding and running out of
self-deceptive reasons until you get closer to the truth. It takes
perseverance.

Sometimes, when a class I am teaching does not go so
well, my first response might be to think that the students are
not interested. It would be easy to leave it at that. By seeing
the students as the cause of a lacklustre class, it lets me off the

hook, when perhaps I didn't engage well with them. As I push myself for the reason why, I realise it was because I didn't pitch the material at the right level. Why? Because I didn't prepare in advance sufficiently. And the reason why? Because, in fact, the topic didn't particularly interest *me*.

EXERCISE 4: Pre-empt your defensive behaviour

1 Think about something that is going on in your life right now that causes you some upset. Perhaps it is a difficult situation at work; imagine you are arriving at work tomorrow morning. Perhaps it is an argument with a friend; imagine you are meeting the friend tomorrow. Whatever the situation is, can you look forward, imagine the event and see yourself rising to the challenges it presents?

2 Play it through in your mind as you would wish it to go. Imagine yourself at your best doing what is needed to overcome the obstacles and resolve the difficulties. What are the strengths and skills within you that you will have to make use of to overcome the situation?

3 Imagine that things turn out well because of your efforts.

4 After the event actually happens, come back to this and compare what you imagined with what actually happened. Did it go as you wished? If not, what made the difference? What can you learn?

EXERCISE 5: Be open to new information

1 Which of the following statements describe you?

- I cherish opportunities to learn about myself.
- I am able to accept my failings and eager to learn from them.
- I am able to receive both compliments and criticism.

2 How many of the above statements would you agree are true for you? The more you agreed with, the more likely you are to be the sort of person who is able to seek to take responsibility for finding out about themselves.
3 Think about the statements above that you disagreed with, and ask yourself what it is that stops you practising them.

EXERCISE 6: Look for the grain of truth

Next time you feel criticised by someone, ask yourself if there is any truth in this, no matter how small. Learn what the truth is. Then ditch the rest of the criticism.

We are all confronted regularly with experiences that challenge us and offer us opportunities to learn about ourselves, but often we walk past such opportunities. For example, the close friend who offers words of warning to us on our new lover: instead of wondering what truth there may be in what she tells us, we turn against our friend. Or a colleague tells us that the new job we have applied for does not suit us; so eager are we for the higher salary that we race ahead, telling ourselves that the colleague speaks only out of jealousy. How much better would it be to stop and think if there is even a grain of truth in what they say? Often there is, and it is worth looking for before we throw out the criticism.

EXERCISE 7: Gain confidence that you can do it

Sometimes we can feel stuck, but when we look back on our lives we can see quickly that we do in fact change and grow.

1 Think of a time in the past that was difficult, challenging or stressful. Don't think of something too recent that you are still going through and which still affects you emotionally, but think of something more distant that, although hard at the time, is now part of your past.

2 What did you learn about yourself from what happened? For example, do you feel you found out about some strengths of character that you didn't know you had? Do you feel wiser as a result?

EXERCISE 8: Don't look back on your life with regrets

Earlier, I introduced a quote from Steve Jobs. Jobs also said how he strove to live each day as if it were his last:

When I was 17, I read a quote that went something like: 'If you live each day as if it was your last, someday you'll most certainly be right.' It made an impression on me, and since then, for the past 33 years, I have looked in the mirror every morning and asked myself: 'If today were the last day of my life, would I want to do what I am about to do today?' And whenever the answer has been 'No' for too many days in a row, I know I need to change something.

Steve Jobs was right. Facing up to the inevitable fact of one's mortality puts our expectations, hopes, fears, ambitions and embarrassments into perspective. Right now, use this moment as an opportunity to look in your own mirror and ask yourself if you are doing what you want to do with your life. Which of the following statements is the one that you most agree with?

- I am doing exactly what I want with my life.
- Most of the time I am doing what I want with my life.
- Some of the time I am doing what I want with my life.
- Most of the time I am not doing what I want with my life.
- None of the time do I do what I want with my life.

Let your answers to these questions be your mirror. To help you begin to think about the direction that you might want to take, it might be helpful to think about when you feel you can be most you and when you feel you can be least you.

EXERCISE 9: Write your mission statement

In the film *Jerry Maguire*, starring Tom Cruise, Maguire is a sports agent who realises that he doesn't like his place in the world – his ambition to succeed materialistically has overtaken his humanity. He doesn't like what he has come to stand for. A turning point has been reached. It is 2 a.m. Maguire sits down at his desk and writes a new manifesto in which caring for his clients and looking after the common good, even if it means loss of revenue, is what he has to do.

All organisations have mission statements stating what they stand for and what they aim to do. As individuals, we all have our own mission statements; however, these are often tucked away in the back of our minds, written years ago when we were children, and we don't even realise we are still living our lives according to these old statements. We need to dig deep within ourselves. Now is an opportunity to do just that. First, think about what your values are, then what your overall aim is. Finally you might list your main objectives. For example, a person dedicated to their family might write something like:

I value compassion in myself and others.

I aim to make a difference in the lives of those I care for.

My objectives are to help my son and daughter find their own way in life; to work enough to be able to support my family but not to be so consumed by work that it takes me away from my family.

EXERCISE 10: Overcome your fear of negative evaluation

As a result of learning to always live to others' rules and expectations, one can develop a powerful fear of being negatively evaluated by others.[3] Would you agree with the following statements?

- I am the sort of person who worries about what other people think of them.
- After I meet someone I usually worry about what they think of me.
- I am the type of person who is concerned about the impression I make on others.

If you agreed with most of these statements, it is likely that your fear of negative evaluation is a barrier for you in being yourself. If that sounds like you:

1 Think about a recent situation in which you were concerned about what other people thought.
2 How did your beliefs influence you in that situation? What did you do because of your beliefs that was helpful to you? What did you do because of your beliefs that was unhelpful to you?

3 If you could go back, what would you like to do
   differently? Take ten minutes to imagine that situation
   and the actions you would take now.

———————————

This chapter will have helped you think about the situations in which you most struggle to take responsibility for your choices, exactly what the choices are that you wish to make, and some of the barriers you face to fully 'owning' yourself. In the next chapter we will turn to the issue of being yourself.

Chapter 10

Step 3 – Be Yourself

Everyone is authentic in their own unique way. Not surprisingly, authentic people try to spend more time doing the things they truly love – the activities that they are passionate about and which make them feel alive. Being less defensive and more open to experience, they are inclined to develop the enduring strengths, interests and inclinations that predispose them to benefit from some activities more than others.

EXERCISE 1: How joined up is your life?

Take time to think about your answers to each of the questions below.

1 What are your passions – the things you enjoy doing, that excite you and give you a sense of flow?
2 What is important to you – what are the values you hold and the things you prioritise?
3 What are you good at – your abilities, talents and strengths?

Now think about how you actually spend your time. Consider a typical week and all your work and leisure activities during that week. How much of the time are you engaging your passions? How much of the time do you spend on activities that are important to you? How often are you doing things that you are good at and that make the most of your abilities, talents and strengths? You might find it useful to look back at a typical week in your diary to think about how you allocate your time.

Now think about those times during the week when you do all three things together – when you are engaging your passions on activities that are important to you and fully using your abilities, talents and strengths. For many people this will only account for a small portion of their time. Can you think of ways in which you can begin to expand this amount of time?

EXERCISE 2: **Practise mindful breathing**

By definition, authentic people are mindful. Mindfulness has long been recognised as a means for improving self-awareness and thereby allowing oneself to make more informed and deliberate choices.

Mindfulness is a topic that has attracted a huge amount of interest in recent years. For the authentic person, mindfulness is more than a way of coping – it is a way of life that helps us to be ourselves.

Below is a one-minute breathing exercise that can be carried out wherever you are sitting comfortably and safely, such as on a train, bus or plane. As the name suggests, it only takes a minute, so it is easy to fit in a bit of mindful breathing a few times a day. Mindfulness exercises help us to get in touch with our bodies and what's going on within us, so don't try these exercises if you need to stay focused on the world around you, such as when driving a car. Get used to one-minute breathing and you will find that it's a useful way to relax in stressful situations and to calm yourself down when you feel tense.

As you become proficient at one-minute breathing, I would encourage you to take it further. Begin to set some time aside. Five or ten minutes once or twice a day, where you sit quietly and observe your breathing, is all you need. At first you may find your mind wandering as thoughts pop into your mind. But as you get more practised at doing this you will find yourself becoming better at simply observing your thoughts as your mind wanders and you will be able to return to simply watching your breathing.

1 First, make sure you are comfortable and safe. Now breathe in slowly through your nose.
2 Hold your breath for a count of six.
3 Slowly breathe out through your mouth, imagining your breath flowing out into the atmosphere.
4 Repeat this sequence ten times. Just focus on your breathing and nothing else for that one minute.

Mindful breathing can be useful at any time during the day when you need to slow down, regain focus, or deal with stressful feelings.

EXERCISE 3: Mindful watching and listening

This is about noticing things in the world around us. In the rush of everyday life, it is easy not to notice what is around us.

1 Choose a tree or a flower that you can see.
2 Watch it for five minutes.
3 Don't do anything else but observe the tree or flower. Notice every aspect.

4 When you are ready, expand your awareness further by closing your eyes and listening for two minutes to all the sounds around you.

EXERCISE 4: Practise mindful activity

Often, when we are doing things, our mind is elsewhere. In the mornings, when you are leaving for work, or dropping the children off at school or whatever you might be doing, you might find yourself getting into the car or already halfway down the street when you wonder to yourself: *Did I lock the door?* Or you might have any number of thoughts that show you weren't aware of what you were doing, so preoccupied were you with thoughts about the day ahead. As you build up your ability to be mindful, you will find yourself introducing it into your everyday life more and more.

1 Choose a daily activity, such as leaving the house in the morning to go to work or going round the supermarket. Your task is to go through your daily actions completely aware of what you are doing and focused on the present moment. The way to do this is to say to yourself, 'I've got a lot on my mind right now, but for the moment I need to focus my attention 100 per cent on what I'm doing right now and do that and nothing else.'

2 If you find your attention wandering as you do these everyday tasks, it might help you if you talk to you yourself as you go to describe what you are doing: 'I'm picking up my bag. Now I'm checking my keys are inside. I'm opening the door. Now I'm locking the door behind me.' Straightforward as that sounds, it will keep you focused on what you are doing and mindful of the present moment.

3 As you get better at being mindful of your daily
   activities, you may begin to also observe what's going
   on inside you as you go through the day. If you can
   observe your feelings from a detached point of view,
   you will not be consumed, in the moment, by the
   feelings themselves. Instead of being at the mercy of
   your emotions, you will become in control of how you
   react to your thoughts.

4 Practise relating to your inner experiences in a new
   and different way. Observe your thoughts as if they are
   words on a screen – simply observe them in a detached
   way. The point is to be able to take a non-judgemental
   approach to engaging with your experiences, to simply
   be curious, open and accepting of our thoughts and
   feelings.

EXERCISE 5: Self-acceptance

How we talk to ourselves is important. Often, we don't even
notice how demanding, coercive and judgemental we are of
ourselves. We need to learn to use compassionate language
with ourselves. Notice when you think in terms of what you
'should', 'ought' or 'have' to do. There are times for these
words, but a lot of the time they could be replaced with phrases
like 'it makes sense to' or 'now is a good time to'. Respect your
own autonomy in life and don't be the person who restricts
your own freedom to choose. Promise yourself to pay attention
to when you hear yourself saying to yourself that you 'should',
'ought' or 'have' to do something and question whether that
really is the case.

Below is a list of statements dealing with your general
feelings about yourself.[4] Which of these would you agree with?

- I appreciate myself as a person even though I'm not perfect.
- If someone criticises what I do, I can learn from that without thinking less of myself.
- If people judge me that is up to them, what matters to me is how I judge myself.

If you generally agree with the above statements, you have a high degree of self-acceptance. If not, you might find it hard to make decisions for yourself, as you need to gain other people's approval.

EXERCISE 6: Pay attention to your interactions with other people

Imagine this scenario. It has been a long and busy day at work. During an earlier meeting you had a tense conversation with a colleague, Bob. You and he have never got on that well and you certainly wouldn't describe yourselves as friends. But, as you think back over the day, you realise that in fact you had misjudged the situation earlier and it was you that had been overly critical of him when actually he hadn't deserved all of that criticism. As you are thinking about this and walking along the corridor on your way to your car for the evening drive home, you bump into Bob, who is also on his way home. You are feeling warm and kindly towards Bob because you realise you have treated him unjustly earlier, so you make more of an effort than usual, 'Goodnight Bob, hope you have a nice evening and see you tomorrow.' Bob glances up, not making eye contact and says, 'You too, safe drive home.'

As you walk to the car you are puzzled. You think about Bob's tone of voice and his body language. What had just happened? Much of our everyday interactions are of this nature with people making socially acceptable conversation that disguise a host of ulterior messages.

Eric Berne introduced a system of therapy known as 'transactional analysis' (TA). This is a complex theoretical system, a portion of which is what is called the 'ego state model'. This consists of three ego states: the child, the parent and the adult. In our child ego state we think and feel in a way like we did when we were children. In our parent ego state we think and feel in a way like those of the significant parental figures from our childhood. In our adult ego state we think and feel in ways that are direct responses to the here-and-now environment.

Any behaviour is driven by the ego state that is in control of the personality at that moment. Normally, Berne argued, we move in and out of these different ego states. We can analyse interpersonal interactions in terms of the communication between individuals at an ego state level of analysis.

Often, at a 'social level', it might appear that we are talking adult to adult, but at the 'psychological level', something else is happening; for example, we are talking parent to child or child to parent. The social level refers to what we say to one another, whereas the psychological level refers to what we really mean. Berne maintained that the psychological message was always the real message, and it was at this psychological level that the course of events was always determined.

As you think about your colleague Bob, you begin to wonder if his communication to you came from a child state. You can't be sure but you think this because you remember how he was walking down the corridor towards you with his head down, almost like a scolded child. Then you wonder about your own ego state. Had you been operating as a controlling parent? That seems to ring a bell for you as you recall how self-satisfied you felt and how patronising you may have come across to Bob earlier in the meeting and even when you said goodnight. As you get into your car, you continue mulling over what just happened but vow that in future you will make more effort to maintain your adult ego state so as to behave differently the next time you meet Bob. You want to be more attentive to when you find yourself switching into either parent or child states. You realise that if you had been in an adult ego state when you met in the corridor you would have taken the opportunity to say sorry and explain how you realised your mistake at the meeting.

Berne's ego state model is a useful way of thinking about authentic communication. Authentic communication in Berne's model is adult to adult. Inauthentic communication is when it looks adult to adult but it is, in fact, ulterior, such as child to parent or parent to child. Authentic people strive to make their communication, both at the social and the psychological level, consistent.

How do we know when we are out of our adult ego state? One tell-tale sign is when we find ourselves not fully listening to the other person with our full attention and with the aim to understand but instead we are judging and evaluating in a way that either approves or disapproves of the other person. Now, of course, there are situations in which it is appropriate to judge and evaluate, such as if we are conducting an interview and we are trying to assess the abilities of a person against some set criteria. But otherwise, it is never the case that in an adult ego state we will judge and evaluate a person as a human being. In an adult ego state we listen with the purpose of understanding the other person's meanings and how they have come to hold the views and opinions they have without judgement. Listening like that is hard work.

1 Think of a recent encounter with someone that left you feeling upset or confused.
2 Work through using Berne's theory to understand what might have actually happened.
3 You may want to talk to the person about what happened. Or it may be that it is appropriate for now

simply to become more practised at using Berne's ego state model to think through your interactions with others.

EXERCISE 7: **Be assertive**

Authentic people are able to be straight down the line with others. Instead of reacting to a challenge with a defensive reaction, they say it like it is in a way that is true to themselves and respectful of other people. One of the problems many of us have is the inability to say no. As we saw earlier, when we are young and finding our way in the world the need to belong and be accepted by others can trump our need for autonomy and agency of our own lives. We want to please our parents. We want to fit in at school. We want the boss to value us. We learn to say yes even when in our hearts we want to say no. In this way we lose touch with ourselves.

Oprah Winfrey writes about how she was 40 years old before she learned to say no. She describes how, because of her reputation, she would be approached by all sorts of people seeking financial help, and it was all too common for her to automatically say yes and get out her cheque book. She realised that this was the result of her own childhood which was abusive and set her up with a fear of rejection, which left her running ragged trying to fulfil others' expectations. She realised this was what she was doing and that she did not have to prove anything to anyone, but, more importantly, she had to accept herself. She tells of how she wrote a few words that she keeps on her desk:

Never again will I do anything for anyone that I do not feel directly from my heart. I will not attend a meeting, make a phone call, write a letter, sponsor or participate in any activity in which every fibre of my being does not resound 'yes'. I will act with the intent to be true to myself.[5]

Oprah Winfrey clearly has some flexibility in her life to stand her ground in a way that most of us don't, because she is a powerful and wealthy person, whereas most of us simply do have to do things we don't want to do. Or do we? The truth is that many of us are a lot more powerful than we dare to let ourselves know, and we do have the capacity to say no more often than we do. Once we realise this we can learn to change.

Next time you are asked to do something, give yourself time to reflect on what it means to you and whether it will be consistent with your values. 'Thank you for asking me. I appreciate the invitation, but I will have to think about it. I will get back to you tomorrow', 'I have thought about your request and I have to say no. It is not something I want to do' – you will find your own words. Yes, your life will begin to change. You may lose friends. But do you want friends who wish you to do things that you don't want to do?

Whether it is friends, your family or your boss, if they are asking you to do things that do not fit in with your values and that you do not wish to do, remember that it is your life and ultimately you choose your actions. At the same time you have to be realistic about the implications of living an authentic life. If, for example, your boss asks you to do something that is completely in keeping with your job description and you don't want to do it, the bigger choice for you is whether you are in the right job. You might think to yourself: *I don't want to do this, but it is what I'm paid to do, so I either do it or I resign and find something else which allows me to be true to myself.*

To be able to be assertive and to say no, we need to be able to listen to our own inner voice to know exactly where we draw the boundaries around us in our lives. It is when our own inner voice is drowned out by others that we become confused about where to draw the line.

EXERCISE 8: **Set boundaries**

This is the tale of the camel's nose. Imagine you are a camel driver in the dusty desert. You are crossing the desert and find yourself in a really bad, windy stretch. You know that there is a sand storm brewing because the camel's nose is twitching, so you stop the train and decide to set up camp. You have just finished putting up your tent and are sitting inside comfortably making a cup of tea when the camel sticks its nose inside the tent. As this is an imaginary story, the camel says to you, 'Hello, how are things in the tent? It is really awful out here in all this sand. Can I just put my nose inside the flap for ten minutes?'

You know that there's a rule that says no camels are allowed inside the tents, but you think to yourself, *What's the harm, it is very windy and after all it's only its nose*. You say to the camel, 'OK, bring your nose inside the tent.' The camel gives you a big smile and sticks its nose inside the tent.

Ten minutes later, the camel puts its eyes and ears inside the tent, saying, 'My throat is so dry and my eyes and ears are full of sand, can I just put my head in for a bit?' You think to yourself: *Well I can understand that – I wouldn't like to be in your shoes*, so you say to the camel, 'Oh all right then.' Twenty minutes later, the camel gives you a big smile and says, 'I must say my neck has a bit of a draught on it and you know what I'm like when I get a chill, so is it OK if I just edge in a bit more?' Seeing the camel's big smile, you say, 'Of course, what harm can that do?'

Well, another 20 minutes later, the camel is trampling all around the tent, knocking over the kettle, getting all tangled up in the ropes and bumping its head on the ceiling and getting quite distressed – and you are outside in the desert, having a really hard time in all that sand.[6] The lesson of this story is: if you don't know your boundaries and assertively stick to them, you will find you get into situations that you realise aren't the ones you would have wished for. You need to know your own boundaries. If you don't know your own boundaries, you can't expect other people to know them. But if you know your boundaries you can be absolutely clear to others what they are, and if they don't respect your boundaries, they don't respect you.

Think about what is acceptable for you in your relationships, whether at home or at work. If in doubt about your answer to a request, always say that you need time to think about it.

EXERCISE 9: Cultivate your dreams by turning them into specific goals[7]

This exercise involves thinking about your life at some point in the future. It could be in a few days, a month, or even several years. The purpose is to help you think through what you want to achieve.

1 Imagine that at this future time all that you hoped for has come true. What does that look like for you?
2 Usually when we look to the future and visualise our ideal lives we don't think about the steps it would take for us to get there. This time, make a list of as many of the goals you can think of that you would have to achieve for that outcome to be true. For example, Adam would love to leave his job and set up his own business. He often fantasises about what that would be like and the freedom it would give him. Adam could do very well in his own business. He certainly has the talent for it and it would allow him to be truer to

himself. It is a good idea, but Adam's strengths are in his creativity and ability to engage with others, not in planning. For that reason, he hasn't thought it through well enough to be able to move his vision forward. If he was to do this, he would see that his list of goals would include: developing a stronger network of contacts in the industry; researching the competition; identifying his unique selling points; developing a brand identity; building a webpage; establishing an initial marketing budget; and securing initial contracts.

3 Having listed your goals, now put them in the most logical order and in a realistic time frame. For example, if your vision is to be healthier and fitter you can't make your vision come true overnight. It will take time. You will need a series of goals involving taking exercise, examining your diet, and dealing with stress or other triggers to unhealthy habits. The timescale may be weeks, months or even years to get to the final vision but by breaking your vision down into specific and achievable goals you will nevertheless find you achieve a sense of accomplishment and reward during this time.

4 Now you will have to tackle each goal in turn and what it will involve. Take the first goal. Break it down into its parts. What has to be done to achieve that goal? For example, imagine your first goal on the list is to lose a stone in weight. What foods do you need to cut back on? Will you decrease your alcohol intake? How about increasing the amount of walking you do each day? For other goals, the steps might not be so straightforward, in which case, ask yourself if you need to seek advice and expertise from others. Do you know who you might ask? If not, how will you go about finding the right person to help you?

5   Having tackled the first goal on your list, move on to
the second goal and work out what steps you will need
to take. Keep going until you have worked through the
steps you need to take to achieve each of your goals.

The above exercise might seem like common sense, but
remarkably few of us actually spend the time we need to visualise
our desired future and to think through the goals we would need
to achieve to make that future happen. Depending on what it
was you decided to visualise, how far into the future it is, and
how important it is to you, you may need to take additional time
to dig down into this exercise, as it really could change your life.
And if you really want to take it seriously you might also consider
enlisting the help of a coach to talk your goals through with. The
next exercise will help you commit to action.

EXERCISE 10: **Make a commitment to new action**

Many of the previous exercises involved thinking about yourself,
your past and your future, but authenticity also involves taking
action. This exercise involves making a commitment to yourself
that you will take action.

1   If you have read this far into the book, ideas will have come
to you about things that you could do differently. It might
be about spending your time doing other things than you
usually would, having that conversation with someone,
or travelling to a place that you have always wanted to
visit, for example. Whatever it is for you, don't let your
motivation for change slip away. Make a commitment that
you will do at least one new thing that challenges you and
takes you out of your comfort zone but which you also
know will probably be in your best interests.

2 Write down what it is you will do and when you will do it.

3 Rate how sure you are that you will do what you have planned, on a scale of 1 to 10, where 1 = not very likely and 10 = I will definitely do this.

4 If you rated the likelihood of you putting into action your new activity at 10, that's great. If less than 10, why was this? What are the barriers to making this activity a 10? What do you have to do to make it a 10? Keep going with this exercise until you have chosen a new activity that feels authentic and which you are able to commit fully to.

5 Make sure that you always have at least one new authentic action to look forward to.

————————

As I said in the introduction to this section of the book, becoming more authentic involves dismantling the self-image that you may, in the past, have tried so hard to preserve. That will take time. The exercises in this and the previous two chapters will help you in your quest to know yourself, own yourself and be yourself. Some exercises you may feel you only need to do once, but others may be worth revisiting time and again. Don't see this as the end to your journey but as a beginning.

In the following chapters I will examine the ways in which you can further build authenticity into your daily life.

PART IV

Authentic Living in the 21st Century

I realize that whatever I have learned is applicable to all of my relationships, not just to working with clients with problems.

Carl R. Rogers

In the chapters that follow, I will show how authenticity can be at the heart of being a parent, how it informs the way in which we approach learning, how we can choose to deal with toxic workplaces, how it can help us to be effective leaders, and how it can help to determine the quality of our relationships. One or more of these topics might be relevant to you right now.

Chapter 11

Nurture Authenticity in Your Children

Authentic parenting is when you do all you can to help your children become who they are, rather than trying to make them be like you, or to live up to some other ideal. To do that you have to work hard to meet your children's needs for agency and for belonging. That means, don't be controlling, instead value your children for who they are.

This is not a message that anything goes and that boundaries do not need to be set for children. Rather, it is an opportunity for parents to learn how to set boundaries without withdrawing their acceptance and love. It is about owning the responsibility that you have for the personal growth of your children, to do all you can to guide, advise and care for them, but without the expectation of getting anything in return.

Your ability to be an authentic parent is limited only by the level of your own authenticity. If you haven't worked through your own conditions of worth and got to understand your own tendencies towards the use of defences, the chances are that you will struggle to be unconditionally accepting of your children. You need to be able to value and accept yourself if you are to be able to provide the same acceptance and unconditional love for others.

Unconditional love

The idea of unconditional positive regard has often been misunderstood as saying that we should praise our children as a way to bolster their self-esteem. Many parents are liberal with their praise, telling their children how wonderful, beautiful or intelligent they are, but this is not what it is about. Praise is only helpful when it is meaningful. Be careful how you praise your children.

Don't be lavish in praising your children about things over which they have no control, such as intelligence, physical attractiveness, or athletic or artistic gifts. Instead, direct your praise to areas over which your children can exert effort and take ownership, such as their attitude to a task, the level of responsibility they assume, their commitment, compassion, generosity to others and so on.[1]

Children who are praised for uncontrollable qualities as compared to their behaviours will persist less following failure; for example, if following a success we praise our children for their intelligence, next time, if they fail, the implication is that they are stupid. That could lead some children to develop a fear of failure in which they become less confident to take on new challenges.

At the same time, when we praise we should do so with an unconditional attitude. Remember we don't want our praise to lead to our children developing conditions of worth. Don't give the message that your love is conditional on them doing something that you want. For example, don't say, 'I love you because you worked hard' or 'I love you because you won the prize'.

If you give those messages, your children will learn that to be loved they must work hard or win prizes. Authentic parents love their children for themselves just as they are.

Observe

All you need to do is observe your children. If your child just put building blocks together for the first time, just say, 'You put the blocks together.' Watch their reaction and you will see for yourself that nothing more needs to be said. With older children, observe the outcome and ask your children what made it happen. Let them tell you what they think they did right.

'You did well. How did you do it?'

'I worked hard.'

'Yes you did work hard.'

Show interest

Observe with interest. Showing interest in your children is important. Many parents misunderstand what it means to show interest and push their interests onto their children. They want their children to take an interest in a particular activity. They may want their children to like the same things that they do. Instead, listen to your children to find out what interests them. Ask your children questions about what they think and feel. Let it be their interests that guide you.

'What made that fun for you?'

'What is it that you like so much about that?'

'What did you enjoy most?'

'What are you looking forward to?'

Allow your children to decide for themselves what they think and how they feel.

Listen to your children

Observe with interest and listen. Listen to your children with the sole purpose of understanding what it is like to be them and what interests them, and then support them to develop their interests. The lesson is that as parents we need to listen at least as much as we talk. You need to help your children think for themselves. You need to look out for their strengths, talents and abilities. For some children, it will be obvious what their passions are, but for others you might need to observe for longer before you realise what they are. Our own expectations can get in the way of us seeing our children for who they are.

Value your children's individuality

Each child is different. Assure your children that you love them just as they are. Give them the freedom to be themselves and not someone that they think you want them to be.

Don't put labels on your children

Don't label your children in ways that restrict their opportunities for growth.

CASE STUDY: *Lisa*

Lisa said, 'My mum always used to say to us that I was the clever one, but my sister, Michelle, was the pretty one.' For Lisa it was like she couldn't be attractive because that was for her sister, and likewise her sister could not be clever.

Let your children tell you who they are.

Tailor your parental style to your child's temperament

You don't want to label your child in ways that restrict their personal growth, but you do want to recognise the ways in which your children might be different. With more than one child you will have to tailor your parental style to their individual temperaments.

CASE STUDY: *Jack and Jamie*

Jack and Jamie are very different. Jack is now 11. He is easy going, intellectual and can easily spend time by himself reading. Jamie is five. He is active, energetic and constantly needs external stimulation. When Jamie was born, his mother, Heather, immediately noticed how different he was from how Jack had been. She was used to Jack, and at first Jamie seemed unusual. 'As soon as he was born he was trying to climb things and without really thinking about it I tried to get him to be more like how Jack had been. It took me a time to realise that he had his own way and I needed to tune into his different needs.'

Accept your children so that you nurture their needs for autonomy and belonging.

Let your children find their own path

Support your children's needs for autonomy and belonging, and they will find their own path in life. This does not imply passively looking on at all that they do, but rather an active hands-on approach. You can get involved to help practically, offer advice and be there for them emotionally, but always do these things in an unconditional way so that offers can be refused without you taking offence. That can be hard for many parents, but once you step over into doing these things conditionally – offering help with strings attached – you are undermining your own efforts to help your children flourish.

In the end, the chances are that your children won't thank you if your love is conditional, as they will hold you responsible for the failures in their life. And the fact is you will have played a role in making those failures come about. You can't determine the path of another person's life without undermining their ability to choose for themselves.

Don't live your life through your children

What many parents do is to relive their own lives again through their children. Certainly, we all learn through life and can look back at where we went wrong and hope to pass on some of that wisdom to our children. But in the same way that it is never possible to step into the same river twice, time changes everything and what was true in your day may not be so any more. As a parent you need to be able to offer your wisdom gently and cautiously in the knowledge that the world changes and the future for your children will not be the same as it was for you.

Be a role model

If you live a predominately authentic life, your children will see that and grow up to derive well-being themselves from eudaimonic ways of living. If they see you grow and learn from experiences, overcome obstacles with wisdom, put effort into activities that give you meaning and purpose and let intrinsic values be your guide, this is what they will learn from you.

Adapt as your children get older

As parents, we also need to adapt to our children as they get older. How we show unconditional love when they are 3 will be different from when they are 13 to when they are 23. Children develop, and it can be heart-breaking for some parents as children move from one stage of life to the next. We might enjoy their toddler years so much that we fail to see that they themselves are leaving those years behind, or moving into young adulthood when we are reluctant to let go of their adolescence; for example, it can be particularly hard for some parents as their children reach their own sexual maturity to accept that this is happening. As such, they may deny the reality to themselves and carry on treating their children as if they were adolescents rather than the teenagers that they have become.

Let your children take age-appropriate responsibility

You need to judge the stage your children are at and let them take as much responsibility for their own lives as is reasonable for them. Just like when they were young and you stopped cutting up their food, know when it is time to let them decide their own bedtime, their choice of friends, their activities, subjects to study and university to attend. By all means advise, but don't control. Give them the benefit of your wisdom but also use your wisdom to know when to step back. Remember, your role is to help your children find their own road in life and learn to be responsible for themselves.

Warren Buffett is one of the richest men in the world, with a fortune estimated at around 36 billion pounds. His son Peter tells of how he asked his father for a loan when he was in his early twenties but was refused and advised to go to the bank.

Now, a quarter of a century later, in an interview, he says he understands why:

> It sounds harsh, but it's actually very loving. It's a show of respect, saying: 'You can do it. I believe in you and if I give you a crutch you are never going to learn how to walk.' That's the way I look at it and I think that's right. I did go to the bank and I got loans for equipment and built my business and worked my tail off to pay the loans off and I would not have done that if somebody was just writing me a cheque.[2]

Of course, for most of us, the advantages Peter Buffett had in life despite this are well beyond our own wildest dreams. Nonetheless, the idea that too much help can actually be detrimental to a young person in finding their own way seems spot on and consistent with the notion that our task as parents is to support the developing autonomy of our offspring.

Understand that their world is not your world

Children will develop passions and interests that their parents simply don't understand. Tastes in fashion and music change. The world of today's teenagers will be different to the world of yesterday's teenagers. As parents, we may not be keeping up with the latest trends, and a cultural gulf can begin to open up between us and our children. It is important that you understand their world and what it looks like from their perspective. Observe and ask questions, respectfully. Get to know their world, but don't go too far to try to enter it yourself.

Don't use your children to compete with other parents

We need to be able to let our children be themselves, which can be difficult when there are so many pressures on us as parents to fit in and even to compete with other parents on the achievements of our children. Our children's achievements, what classes they attend after school, what awards they have been given, and so on, are not currency for you to compete with your neighbours or other parents at the school gates.

Help others to be free to learn

Most people's view of education is wrong. They think education is about someone standing at the front of a class explaining things to those in front of them. Unfortunately, a lot of teachers seem to think this, too. It is an outdated notion that the role of the teacher is to fill the heads of their pupils with stuff from a textbook that they may have only just read themselves.

Many experts in child development and education have, however, reached a different conclusion. Young people do not have to be forced to learn and grow. It is a natural process. Learning can be an intrinsically motivating activity. As an educator, it is important therefore that you discover ways to find, cultivate and sustain children's intrinsic motivations – the things that really inspire and interest them personally, rather than the things that others expect of them. You need to nurture children's experiences of agency and their ability to form their own relationships.[3]

Carl Rogers said, 'The only man who is educated is the man who has learned how to learn; the man who has learned how to adapt and change; the man who has realized that no knowledge is secure, that only the process of seeking knowledge gives a basis for security.'[4] One of Rogers's major projects was to apply the ideas of authenticity to education, and in his book *Freedom to Learn* he sets out his philosophy of education: that human beings have a natural urge to learn, that this most readily happens when the subject matter is perceived as relevant to the student, that learning is best achieved by doing, that the most lasting learning takes place in an atmosphere of freedom.

In the modern world, information is readily available in a way that it wasn't in the past. There is very little information that one person can impart to another that they couldn't get for themselves.

Education should be about the freedom for people to explore and develop their own interests. Students who are not motivated to learn and not interested in a subject will not do well. Coercing people to learn about something that doesn't interest them and which doesn't play to their interests or strengths wastes everyone's time and leaves the pupil disheartened and feeling like a failure. That seems to be what is happening in the education system as it becomes more of an exam factory for children rather than providing them with the opportunity to grow and develop their own unique strengths.

Let children be guided by their own interests

Parents need to understand that the pressures on children are detrimental to them and schools are not necessarily being effective in helping their child to flourish. Young people need to find something that captures their curiosity that they will be passionate about. The rest will then take care of itself, as long as their needs for autonomy and belonging are met, giving them the freedom to pursue their subject.

The research is clear that children will do better when given the autonomy to find their own direction. The same is true for students of all ages, be they at infant school or young men and women entering university.

Many scientific studies have confirmed the importance of having our basic needs satisfied, regardless of culture, age or personality type. In one study, for example, Ken Sheldon, from the Department of Psychological Sciences at the University of Missouri, and Lawrence Krieger, at Florida State University College of Law, followed a new intake of law students at two universities throughout their law-school careers.[5] Both schools admitted well-qualified candidates and asked for essentially the same entry grades, but they differed in their educational philosophies. Both schools were initially experienced by students as equally good at meeting their needs, but during the first year this changed, and one school was experienced by students as meeting their basic psychological needs better than the other. These students went on to do better academically, be more motivated in their careers and show greater overall well-being.

The role of the educator is not only to impart their knowledge. That may be part of what they do, but the main thing that they can do is to provide their students with the freedom to learn; that is to say, to give them the resources that they will need to support their needs, as determined by them.

W. Timothy Gallwey, a one-time tennis player and coach, in his book *The Inner Game of Tennis* said, 'As a new pro, I too was guilty of over teaching, but one day when I was in a relaxed mood, I began saying less and noticing more. Errors that I saw but I didn't mention were correcting themselves without the student ever knowing he had made them.'[6]

He goes on to describe how individuals have a natural propensity towards learning and mastering new skills, but that too much self-talk and instructions from others can drown out the inner wisdom of the human organism. 'The first skill to learn is the art of letting go of the human inclination to judge ourselves and our performance as either good or bad.'[7]

When we plant a rose seed in the earth, we notice that it is small, but we do not criticize it as 'rootless and stemless.' We treat it as a seed, giving it the water and nourishment required of a seed ... Within it, at all times, it contains its whole potential. It seems to be constantly in the process of change; yet at each stage, at each moment, it is perfectly all right as it is.[8]

Chapter 12

Overcome Toxic Workplaces and Develop Leadership Through Authenticity

Relationships at work can be complicated and difficult at times, and occasionally they can become toxic. Whether we are part of a team or in a leadership position, we will be at our best and most effective when we are authentic in our relationships with others.

Heal the toxic workplace

Sadly, many of us work in organisations that are toxic insofar as employees feel constantly under stress, wishing for a change in career and are even bullied. It is easy to think that bullying is something that happens only to children, but the sad truth is that it is all too common in the workplace. Ask yourself: on Sunday evening, do you dread going to work the next day? Do you ruminate constantly about work even when you are at home? Do you have problems sleeping because of worry and fear? Are you relieved when you are ill because you have a reason not to go to work? When you are not at work, do you do things to try to stop thinking about work, like drinking too much? Do you feel exhausted and run down a lot of the time? If you said yes to any of these, the chances are that your workplace is toxic.

In toxic workplaces there is often an atmosphere of bullying. As adults we can be reluctant to admit that bullying is taking place, but given the consequences for our careers, health and mental well-being it is important that we recognise it for what it is. The problem is that often bullying at work is far more subtle than when we were children. Whereas children might engage in more direct forms of bullying such as name calling and physical violence, adult bullies are more likely to use indirect methods that are harder to identify and, most importantly, to show evidence for. Commonly, workplace bullies use micro-management in such a way that to an observer it simply looks like they are doing their job, but to those on the receiving end the effects are debilitating. The first step is to realise what is happening. Some of the tell-tale signs of indirect bullying are when:

- When others create situations that leave you with a feeling of shame and humiliation
- When others magnify your mistakes beyond what is reasonable
- When others spread rumours about you that are not true
- When others do things that stop other colleagues talking with you
- When others never leave you to get on with your job but constantly interfere

Sometimes bullies don't know they are bullies, but they behave in these ways because they are poor leaders. A good leader will always have a quiet word with you, and support your learning and development, and they will help you find solutions for yourself when things are not going well. A good leader will help you to understand and take control of your work. Not everyone has these skills, however, and it might be that when the bully better understands what they are doing they will change. At other times, however, bullies are just that. Talking to them directly about their behaviour is only likely to cause more problems. They may have low self-worth and bullying is their way to make themselves feel more worthy. Too often they are people who are themselves ill-equipped for the job they are doing, and by putting the spotlight on others they hope to avoid their own inadequacies being exposed. When involved in selecting new staff, rather than appointing the best person for the job, they will choose someone of less talent who will not overshadow them. They may have deep-seated personality issues that mean they are unable to self-reflect on what they are doing.

Of course, if there is clear evidence of bullying then you should consult your company policy and talk to the right people about what is happening. It might also be wise to begin looking for new employment.

Nevertheless, it is rarely that things get sorted so easily or that change can be brought about quickly. In the meantime we can get caught up in our own negative feelings and defences, which add fuel to the fire. After a while, we are contributing to making the workplace toxic ourselves. As time passes, it might even be hard to know how it all started and whether you yourself have helped to create the toxic workplace.

CASE STUDY: *Edwina*

This is what happened to Edwina. With a controlling personality she was unsuited to a recent promotion, which put her in a leadership position. While new to the role and learning the ropes she made many mistakes.

Those around her experienced her as manipulative and
bullying and begin to react defensively. In turn, Edwina
herself experienced their reactions as offensive and
began to experience herself as the victim, even going so
far as to begin documenting others' bullying behaviours
towards her.

Toxic workplaces are full of confusion, and people's judgements
become clouded. Conversations can often be fraught, and pressure can be put on us to respond immediately. Be prepared to
say that you need time to think over an issue and that you will
come back with an answer later. Your aim is to approach situations authentically:

- Try to empathise with others. What's it like to be in their
  shoes?
- Work out what you can do to support the needs of others
- Let others know what they can do to support your needs
- Be assertive but not aggressive in your dealings with others
- Be clear about your boundaries; know which issues are
  your responsibility

Be a catalyst for change. It might just work, and along the way
you will make your own life less stressful in the meantime.

Develop authentic leadership

Some of us have the pleasure to spend our working lives in
organisations that do their best to facilitate employee well-
being. These are organisations that know that if they can get the
best out of their employees everyone benefits. They know that
the key is good management and executive leadership.

Academics in business schools have long been interested in what makes a good leader. This is what businesses want to know. As employees and leaders, we have our own ideas of what we need to look like to be a leader. From many studies across decades the answer is that there is no one style of leadership. Good leaders are varied in the ways they enact their personalities.

Interest by psychologists in authentic leadership has its roots in the earlier work of Carl Rogers and the humanistic psychologists, and more recently positive psychology. Authenticity means that our behaviour comes from deep within us, where we are true to ourselves. Authentic leaders are able to consider multiple sides of an issue and different perspectives so that they can assess information in a balanced way and convey their feelings and values without seeming manipulative. We can all learn to express ourselves in ways that achieve this, such as by actively listening to people, inquiring about what is happening in their lives and speaking truthfully about our own experiences while staying in the present moment. By using these skills, leaders can reveal themselves authentically and relate to others; and in so doing create nurturing environments for their followers that foster positive psychological capacities.

Nurture others to take responsibility

What is important is helping people develop their self-determination, to find their own solutions and foster the best in themselves. At first glance this can look like the opposite of leadership because many people who describe themselves as leaders seem to do the opposite, as in the case of Edwina, whom we met earlier. Edwina talks about herself as a leader. In her middle-management role she would tell people not only what to do, but how to do it. Colleagues felt undermined, devalued and unsupported by her; however, the senior management of the organisation thought she was doing her job well because they too thought of leadership as telling people what to do.

The paradox was that those who worked under Edwina were not functioning well, due to sick-leave absences, lack of motivation and loss of collegiality, which were the result of her authoritarian management. Ironically, to senior management, it looked like the solution was more micro-management.

Authentic leadership on the other hand seeks to support people's own direction and nurture their motivations. Authentic leadership that has the power to transform has four elements:[9]

The first is idealised influence This is when leaders are guided by their moral commitment to do the right thing in terms of their employees, themselves and other stakeholders.

The second is inspirational motivation This is when leaders inspire their followers to be their best and to achieve greater heights than they thought were possible and inspire self-efficacy.

The third is intellectual stimulation This is when the leader is able to step back and not provide all the answers but challenge others to work out solutions for themselves and help them see things differently.

The fourth is individualised consideration This is when leaders empathise, listen and genuinely care for others and cherish the relationship that develops.

The paradox is, however, that unless you know what to look for in a leader you wouldn't know the authentic leader was leading. The authentic leader does not fit the traditional stereotype of the leader.

Typically, people who are not able to lead authentically spend their time trying to look like leaders. Instead of idealised influence, they want to please those senior to themselves, even when it means making the wrong choices. Instead of the inspirational motivation of others, they want to be seen to shine themselves, even when it means keeping others in the shadows. Instead of intellectual stimulation, they want to be seen as having the answers themselves, even when it means disempowering others. Instead of individualised consideration, they want to be seen to be caring, even when by doing so it detracts from the actual care given.

In this way, there is a downward spiral of employee well-being, productivity and morale as more of the same dysfunctional style of leadership is heaped on to solve the problems that it has itself created.

If an organisation has a problem in leadership, it always starts from the top. It is vital that the top person understands what authentic leadership looks like. If they do, it will trickle down throughout the organisation.

Your role of leader is underpinned by how you are as a person

Being an authentic leader is not what you *say* you are; it is *what you are.*

To be an authentic leader involves knowing yourself, owning yourself and being yourself. It is hard to be a good leader if you are not authentic. Generally speaking, the best leaders are authentic, but being authentic will not guarantee that you are a great leader. But you can learn to be a better leader.

Successful senior executives often have coaches to help them keep on track with their performance. The field of executive coaching has exploded over the past decade in both the US and the UK.[10] Twenty years ago, the field was just beginning to take off, but now what we do is well established within organisations, and coaching skills are taught in business schools.

The job is to help leaders widen their repertoire of behaviours, attitudes and mindsets. Executive coaching is not about giving advice or telling people what to do differently; it is designed to help people release the talents, abilities and strengths within them – to become more of who they are. This might be in a one-off consultation for a particular task, a few sessions focusing on specific performance-enhancement issues or open-ended 'developmental' contracts where the aim is to help the organisation move through a series of transitions. The benefits of executive coaching to organisations are tremendous. Leadership coaching also, paradoxically, assists leaders to grapple with the inevitable negative, toxic or near-impossible demands of business life. Just having space to think and vent can restore equilibrium.

Chapter 13

Nurture Authentic Relationships

Throughout this book I have talked about the importance of relationships in providing us with the right environment to foster authenticity and good mental health. Relationships that are unconditional, genuine and empathic help us to bring the best out in ourselves. In such relationships we flourish. When we are truly valued and accepted for who we are, we aspire to be more than we are. Not surprisingly, psychologists tend to promote the idea that people need to develop their relationships as a way to find happiness in life. What is rarely pointed out, however, is the scarcity of such relationships. The fact is that on a day-to-day basis most of our relationships are controlling, false and lacking in understanding.

What we need are relationships that are unconditional, genuine and empathic. We can learn to nurture our relationships.

Listen to other people better

Begin to ask more questions in your relationship. How was your day? How did you feel about that? But the most important thing to do when you ask a question is to listen to the answer. We all know people whose eyes seem to glaze over as you talk to them, and you feel that they are not listening to you but simply waiting for their turn to talk. In fact, many people don't even wait for a turn to talk but barge straight in. Everyone can, however, learn to be a better listener.

Listening is so important if we want to be authentic in our dealings with others. More often we listen to people with the intention that we should change them in some way by getting them to see the situation as we do. As such we argue with them, plead, scold, encourage, manipulate, insult or whatever else might work to get the other person to see things as we do. The reason we do this is that disagreements and conflicting views can be stressful for us unless we are authentic in ourselves, in which case we have no desire to change other people. In fact, the more authentic we are ourselves the more able we are to tolerate ambiguity, conflict, disagreement and even to cherish it as an opportunity to challenge ourselves and our own views.

Authentic people can be confronted with challenges without feeling threatened and having to defend themselves. For many people this is not the case. Even a disagreement over something trivial can be threatening to people who are alienated from themselves and who quickly swing into defensive mode. And, as we know, attack is often the best form of defence.

> Jill: 'I asked you to phone the bank yesterday but you
>   haven't.'
> Jack: 'Are you starting on me now when I've just come
>   in from work – and what have *you* done all day
>   anyway?'

I think you can imagine how the rest of the evening unfolds for Jack and Jill.

As you move towards becoming more authentic, your

relationships will improve because you will find yourself becoming a better communicator.

Authentic people are good listeners. They don't pretend to listen while waiting their turn to talk. They do listen, because whatever you say won't be felt as a challenge to them personally. They are aware of what's going on inside themselves emotionally. They will want to understand better your point of view and how you are feeling and will ask questions and take responsibility for their actions.

Jill: I asked you to phone the bank yesterday but you haven't.'

Jack: 'I know you did and I haven't. I completely forgot, and now that you remind me I feel a bit annoyed at myself. You sound a bit annoyed at me too?'

Promise yourself that the next time you are talking to someone and you find yourself rehearsing what you are going to say while the other person is still talking, that you will stop and just listen to them. Watch them carefully and take in each and every word. Work hard to understand what they mean. Authentic listening involves three aspects:

First, be aware of what's going on within you It involves the awareness of what is going on inside yourself. Our own thoughts bubble up and colour the ways we interpret what the other person is saying; for example, in a counselling session Siobhan is talking about the death of her brother, but as I listen I begin to feel angry at the car driver who killed him, but in becoming angry I completely miss that Siobhan is actually telling me about her journey towards forgiveness. I need to be aware of what is going on inside me and, as my own thoughts bubble up, I need to be able to put them back in a box, put the lid on it and listen to what she is telling me. Put your own thoughts to one side so that your attention is completely on the other person while they are speaking.

Second, see things from the other person's point of view It requires the ability to tune in to the other person's world view and see things from their point of view. Once we have put our own stuff away and are no longer focused on ourselves, we can truly pay attention to what the other person is telling us, but it is not just the words that we need to be attentive to but what it is like for that person right now within them – all their feelings and meanings. Try to imagine yourself in the shoes of the other person. Look at how they are sitting, their posture, listen to the tone of their voice and imagine what it feels like to be in their shoes right now. Try to understand not only what they are saying but how they are feeling as they are saying it.

Third, listen without wanting to change It involves the ability to listen without wanting to change anything about the person. As we step into the other person's world and begin to see things from their point of view, we might wish that things were different in some way for that person, but to authentically listen we need to do so without trying to make things different. Listening is not the same as giving advice to people. Listen without trying to solve any problems or giving advice in any way. Listen with the intention of understanding. Don't interrupt. If you feel the need to interrupt, ask yourself why, and unless it's to clarify your understanding, then don't.

Some dos and don'ts of authentic listening

When you finally have your space to speak, check that you understand what you have just heard. Let the other person know that you are listening, not by telling them you are, but by showing them: paraphrase what you have heard them say, but in a way that is open to correction and clarification. The chances are that you will have caught some of what has been said, missed other aspects and even misunderstood other parts. Summarising what the person has said and being open to hearing how you have not understood everything exactly is the art of authentic listening.

Three expectations of friendship

We also need others to offer us relationships that are genuine and allow us to flourish. Think about your own expectations of your friendships:

Do I expect others to be genuine with me? Do you put up with lies and half-truths from your friends? Do you sometimes feel like you are their back-up plan? Raise your expectations and put your energy into those relationships that are genuine and truly respectful of you.

Do I expect my friends to be unconditional with me? Do you ever feel that your friends only love you if you are the person that they want you to be? Friends should love you just as you are and be pleased when good things happen to you.

Do I expect my friends to be interested and caring of me? Do you feel that your friends try to see things from your point of view? Or do they try to convince you to see things in the same way as they do? Friends should cherish you and how you see things.

Relationships that don't have these qualities will be experienced as controlling. In controlling relationships we may feel ourselves under pressure to make decisions that we don't feel ready to

make, or do things that we don't want to do. In authentic relationships you should expect the space and the support to work
things out.

Strengthen loving relationships

It is in our closest relationships that we can expect to be our
most authentic. Most of us yearn to be in close loving relationships in which we feel cared for and valued, and to feel able to
care for and value our partner. What is it that happens that
makes it so hard to get it right?

For a start, most of us enter into relationships with unrealistic expectations based on fantasy. Often, people get together
in the first place from a position of vulnerability, thinking that
they can find happiness in the other person. Surrounded by
images of men and women with perfect bodies and perfect
lives, in magazines, television and the internet, a real person
can be a let-down. Then there is the fantasy of living together.
Many people plan to live together, but the finishing line in
their dreams is the day when they move in together. The next
morning they wonder what's next, as their life together hasn't
been thought through. Until we are mature enough to know the
realities of life, and to know ourselves well enough and what
we truly want out of our lives and from our partners, our relationships are likely to be doomed to end in separation, divorce
and misery.

Most of the time, in many relationships the communication
between the people involved simply is not authentic. We bring
our defences into play. Loving relationships demand openness,
transparency and deep honesty with each other in which the
bond that develops is genuinely respectful and appreciative of
the other just as they are.

Sexual intimacy

We are sexual beings and require close supportive relationships in which to be ourselves. One of the most difficult areas for communication is sex. Often people are frightened to talk about what they like, to ask what the other person likes and to be fully naked in front of the other, not just physically but emotionally too. Without these conditions, sexual intimacy becomes a façade.

Problems arise for people when their own sexuality or that of their partner is distorted in such a way through denial, repression or some other defence that prevents them from truly knowing themselves as sexual beings. It may be, and this is most commonly in men, that a person protects him or herself from intimacy, perhaps by objectifying their partner as a thing rather than a person; for example, this might involve needing to engage in sexual activity from behind the lens of a camera during the sexual act. For others it might be that they perceive sexual intimacy as sinful in some way and as something to be ashamed of. In these ways the sexual act does not build intimacy and connection.

In an authentic sexually intimate relationship you will feel no need to be ashamed of yourself and all your physical and emotional scars, but you will feel accepted for who you are. Sexual intimacy is part of a loving relationship for most people. Its absence in a relationship, or the inability of the couple to find an agreeable compatibility, can be distressing. Often it is the absence of a satisfactory sexual intimacy which is actually at the root of other problems that arise. Some go through life without ever fully experiencing a truly loving sexual relationship.

Sex is often thought of as a means for obtaining pleasure, and so it can be, but it can also be much more than that. Authentic sexual intimacy will make you feel:

- Alive
- That you are valued
- That you have been seen for who you are
- That you are OK to be you
- That you are cared for
- That you are deeply connected
- That you are desirable
- That you are loved

If that is not how it is for you, then think about whether you can make changes in your relationship.

Some dos and don'ts of building a loving relationship

- Don't avoid discussing issues that are troubling you. Set time aside to talk.
- Talk about the rules of your relationship and be clear to each other what your boundaries are.
- Don't think that strong relationships are effortless.
- Relationships are always changing, and a healthy authentic relationship will not be static but always evolving into something different. Do be open to change.
- Don't assume you know what your partner is thinking.
- Do ask for feedback from your partner about how things are going for them, and listen with a genuine curiosity to hear their point of view.
- Don't assume you understand what your partner means.
- Do be an active listener, by checking that you understand what the other is telling you.
- Don't get bogged down in your own point of view.
- Do ask yourself what are the other ways to look at a situation.
- Don't talk over the other person.

- Do pause before speaking and learn to be comfortable with silence to be sure the other person has space to think and say what they want to.
- Don't always be telling the other person how things ought to be.
- Do ask questions rather than always telling.
- Don't expect the other person to be more than they are.

Chapter 14

Conclusion

Earlier, I introduced the authenticity formula, which consists of knowing yourself, owning yourself and being yourself. It is the combination of these three elements that makes for authentic living.

Become familiar with yourself, get to know who you are, what your deep-seated assumptions about yourself are, and then learn to be able to listen to your inner voice of wisdom, take responsibility for your choices and your actions and then, as you gain in confidence that you know yourself and own yourself, be yourself.

Our own authenticity arises best when we are in relationships that support our agency and belongingness – so do the same for others as you would like them to do for you. Develop an unconditionally regarding attitude towards others.

You can change, but you might not achieve all you want overnight. For most of us, making a genuine life transition may take some time. Perhaps it could be a year or more before you see your life as having turned around in a completely new direction; however, don't let that discourage you. You can start living more authentically right now, moment by moment. It is through a gentle tilt of the rudder now that you will be taken towards a completely different destination later on.

A manifesto for authentic living

This summary of the main points of this book is a reminder of how to take authenticity in your life forward.

With yourself

1 Know your own boundaries and be clear to others what is acceptable to you and what isn't.
2 Use each and every challenge in life as an opportunity to learn about yourself.
3 Be aware of how you feel in the moment and question why those feelings have come about.
4 Listen carefully to your initial gut reactions and what it is you are telling yourself. Try to distinguish your inner voice of wisdom.
5 Learn to accept yourself just as you are.

With others

1 Don't focus on what others lack; do something to help nurture the talents and strengths that they have.
2 Don't keep others down; do point out the potential that they have to reach new heights.
3 Don't try to make people be more like you; do help them become more of who they are.
4 Don't be controlling with others, but always think of how best to support their unique directions in life.
5 Try to understand other people's perspectives on life and listen carefully. Accept that other people are entitled to their view, even if it is different from yours.

This book can be your guide, but it is up to you how much commitment you bring to it. Learning about authenticity is only the first step. To be authentic requires courage to be honest with ourselves and also with others. That can be risky, as other people may not like us to change, particularly if we are beginning to challenge their power over us, which, as we have seen, is one of the barriers to overcome on our quest to be ourselves.

For some, reading this book might have opened up deeper issues that deserve greater exploration than is possible by yourself. Appendix I includes a questionnaire that you can use to evaluate your well-being. Very low scores in the questionnaire might indicate that you would find it useful to seek professional help. You might consider seeking help from a psychological therapist or coach who can help you learn about yourself, set your boundaries and get to grips with difficult emotions. Appendix II offers some advice on seeking help.

The vision of authenticity

Every year, millions of prescriptions are written out for pills to help us manage problems of stress, depression and anxiety. There has been a dramatic increase in the use of prescription medicine, so you might expect rates of mental health problems to be falling, but this does not seem to be the case. Indeed, the opposite seems to be true, with some estimates even suggesting that one in four people suffer from mental health problems each year.[11]

Should we be concerned about the rise in prescription medication to help people deal with their mental health problems? Many are critical of the traditional view of psychiatry that problems are caused by chemical imbalances and question the evidence for the use of medication as the preferred form of treatment.[12] Richard Bentall, the author of *Doctoring the Mind* said, 'The pharmaceutical industry has had a terrible impact on mental health care, not only by peddling medicines that, on careful examination, are not much more effective than snake oil.' [13]

If we understand many of our problems in living, not as chemical imbalances but as having been caused by the lack of authenticity, we are more in control of the solutions. There is much in the modern world that serves to alienate us from ourselves and each other, that discourages us from taking ownership of ourselves, and that is detrimental to our search for authenticity. Our education system is limited in the extent to which it is able to fully support children to flourish to be their best. Sadly, many children fall by the wayside, not having the chance to find out about themselves and what they can excel at.

There are people who have so far in their lives failed to develop their own potentialities in life. One reason for this, which strikes to the heart of this book, is that we don't value all potentialities equally. The truth is that Western society most highly values qualities of leadership, power and wealth creation, but as individuals the values we actually hold most dear are those that preserve and enhance the welfare of people and lead to independent thought and freedom of action. [14]

For sure, at any given time in history, some qualities are more desirable for a society than at other times, and these come to be more richly rewarded. But such necessity needs to be balanced with the viewpoint of authenticity, which is that everyone's strengths and talents should be nurtured and rewarded. A truly rich and rewarding society to live in is one in which everyone can find a place in it to be at their best.

The world is always changing. Young people today face new pressures of social media (communication technologies such as Twitter, Instagram and Snapchat), the psychological effects of which – although widely debated – are still little understood. It also seems that these new technologies have increased the pressure on people to present an enhanced image of themselves to the world.[15] The dark side of these new technologies is shown by the reported suicides of schoolchildren following online abuse and sexual harassment and the use of the internet to objectify sexuality.

Perhaps we need authenticity more than ever. It is becoming harder to live authentic lives as public spaces become eroded unless we have the finances and status to gain entry. As freedoms are eroded, so too is our chance of an authentic life. We increasingly present ourselves to the world as an electronic image. Technologies that can watch us at a distance are ever present. Costs of living increase making us ever more insecure in our ability to look after ourselves and our families. Changes in employment practices exploit us and restrict our opportunities to be ourselves.

Perhaps there is also hope in the new technologies. As well as the dangers of the new technologies they also offer fresh opportunities for people to connect with one another in ways that can foster authenticity. Young people can find forums that allow them to explore their understanding of themselves. Individuals now have the opportunity to come together with one voice. It was social media that helped to facilitate collective action such as the anti-capitalist protests of 2011. Distances between people are broken down, allowing connections to be made between people from across the world.

Challenges to thinking from the past

Another source of hope comes from how traditional views on gender identity are being challenged. Many people have always felt uncomfortable with having to categorise themselves as either gay or straight and welcome new ways of thinking that embrace the idea that gender identity may be much more fluid.

The more we can resist wanting to put people into categories but accept them for who they are the more they will be free to be themselves.

The idea of promoting authenticity challenges the traditional approach of psychology and psychiatry. By and large, psychologists and psychiatrists are interested in reducing emotional suffering and increasing the amount of happiness and pleasure in a person's life – the so-called hedonic orientation. All these aspects are important, but, as we have seen, a fuller consideration of human experience tells us that a hedonic orientation is only part of the wider landscape of well-being.

The wider landscape includes our having a sense of meaning and purpose, mastery and control and self-acceptance, as well as intimate and rewarding relationships and opportunities to develop our strengths and pursue the best in ourselves – the eudaimonic orientation. Conventional psychological therapies and psychiatric medications are hedonic interventions that aim to make us feel better. The latest research shows that psychologists and psychiatrists who ignore the eudaimonic aspects of well-being may do so at the cost of their patients.[16] Authenticity should be at the heart of the helping professions.

CASE STUDY: *Kim*

Kim is a 55-year-old woman who is employed as a cleaner in a large national organisation. She suffers from exhaustion and depression owing to the increasing demands of her employer. It seems forward-looking that her employer runs a counselling programme for staff. But the programme is not concerned with the actual demands on Kim and whether they are realistic, only with helping her find more adaptive ways of coping with her work stress.

Mental health professionals use cognitive-behavioural therapy to show people how to deal with their negative thoughts. At the core of this therapy is the idea that problems in living arise from dysfunctional thinking. This is often true, but life has changed a lot in the 40 years since cognitive-behavioural therapy was developed. In today's world, situational pressures are ever more intense. Therapy may not always recognise the very real pressures on people. We also need to recognise that sometimes it is the situation that needs to change and not the person. If we don't, then therapists are in danger of being part of the problem rather than the solution.

Mental health specialists call for greater resources to be put into their services and the employment of ever more counsellors, psychologists and psychiatrists. But the biggest obstacle to well-being is that we do not do enough to create nurturing environments for people such that we design our systems of parenting, schooling, education and employment so as to nurture the actualisation of people's potentials and prevent mental health problems from arising in the first place. We should not be waiting to address problems reactively in our clinics. We should be using our new knowledge of authenticity now to design our vision for families, schooling and societies. To nurture authenticity, teachers, educators, psychologists and leaders need to provide people with the environments and ability to select their direction in life and to find the right ways for them to be autonomous in society.

If people's problems arise because of poverty, corruption, poor education, unequal social systems and so on, then therapy after the fact is simply not the answer, because it is the social systems that need to be changed. Providing psychotherapy for depressed people whose lives are blighted by poor housing, illness, poverty and so on while ignoring their very real circumstances would seem misguided. On the other hand, nurturing people's authenticity means that they will be more likely to stand up for themselves, act with integrity, be assertive and become part of the solution themselves through protest and political action.[17]

Building authenticity into people's lives

Authenticity is a dangerous idea. When people are authentic they can be awkward, questioning of the status quo and reluctant to be pawns for someone else. Noam Chomsky said:

> every form of authority and domination and hierarchy, every authoritarian structure, has to prove that it's justified – it has no prior justification ... And when you look, most of the time these authority structures have no justification ... they're just there in order to preserve certain structures of power and domination, and the people at the top.[18]

Authentic people strive to have power over their own lives and so will always ask those who assume power over them to justify it. The more authentic we are, the more we, as individuals, will demand authenticity in our institutions and leaders.

The past decade has seen attempts by some psychologists to take their work out of the clinic and apply it more widely in the real world. This has been met with huge success, as the topic of happiness has captured the imagination of governments across the Western world.[19] In April 2012, the UK's Office for National Statistics introduced the first official happiness index. People were asked to rate their well-being on the following four questions, on a scale of 0 to 10: 'How satisfied are you with your life nowadays?', 'How happy did you feel yesterday?', 'How anxious did you feel yesterday?' and 'To what extent do you feel the things you do in your life are worthwhile?'

By using such questions, happiness can be measured in order to assess how public policies affect well-being. Research shows that the world's happiest countries are in northern Europe (Denmark, Norway, Finland, the Netherlands) and the most miserable are in Africa (Togo, Benin, the Central African Republic and Sierra Leone).[20]

Armed with such information, governments can introduce policies for happiness. But we need to recognise what Viktor Frankl[21] said many years ago, that 'Happiness cannot be pursued: it must ensue. One must have a reason to be happy. Once the reason is found, however, one becomes happy automatically.' [22] Likewise, the great philosopher John Stuart Mill also believed that the only people who are happy are those who 'have their minds fixed on some object other than their own happiness; on the happiness of others, on the improvement of mankind, even on some art or pursuit, followed not as a means, but as itself an ideal end'.

My proposal is that alongside any such happiness index should be an authenticity index: to what extent do people feel that they can be themselves, have had their strengths, talents and abilities nurtured and also that they belong in society and have a sense of agency and autonomy in their lives. Rather than happiness, these are the questions that I think we need to ask and which should provide the compass point of public policy. The quest for authenticity should be at the heart of everything we do.

How Happy Are You?

Positive psychologists have come to recognise that well-being is more than the absence of psychological problems, it is also the presence of such states as happiness and contentment. But until recently most psychological tests did not ask about the presence of such positive states. In order to assess well-being in this broader sense, my colleague John Maltby and I developed the following questionnaire.[1]

A number of statements that people have made to describe how they feel is given overleaf. Please read each one and circle the number in the box which best describes how frequently you felt that way in the past seven days, including today. Some statements describe positive feelings and some describe negative feelings. You may have experienced both positive and negative feelings at different times during the past seven days.

		Never	Rarely	Sometimes	Often
1	I felt dissatisfied with my life	3	2	1	0
2	I felt happy	0	1	2	3
3	I felt cheerless	3	2	1	0
4	I felt pleased with the way I am	0	1	2	3
5	I felt that life was enjoyable	0	1	2	3
6	I felt that life was meaningless	3	2	1	0
7	I felt content	0	1	2	3
8	I felt tense	3	2	1	0
9	I felt calm	0	1	2	3
10	I felt relaxed	0	1	2	3
11	I felt upset	3	2	1	0
12	I felt worried	3	2	1	0

To calculate your level of well-being, add up all the numbers you have circled. The lowest score that is possible on this questionnaire is 0. The highest score possible is 36. Most people score between 18 and 28. It is likely that you have scored somewhere in between these numbers.

Score:
18 or below: your level of well-being suggests that you may be experiencing some problems in your life right now.
Above 28: indicates relatively high levels of well-being.

Of course, such tests as the one above, when taken on their own and when not administered by a trained psychologist, can only ever be used as rough-and-ready guides to our well-being. Nonetheless, if you scored very low on the questionnaire it might be worth considering seeking formal professional advice from a trained psychological therapist. You can find details on seeking help in Appendix II.

Some Advice on Seeking Help

Psychological therapies

The fact is that therapists, generally speaking, don't know what's best for you. You might go into therapy expecting answers to questions. Should I take this job? Should I go ahead with divorce? Therapists can't answer this for you. Therapists are not able to read minds, see into the future or know what path in life is best for their clients.

Good therapy is about helping you to think for yourself. A good therapist will listen attentively, try to understand your predicament, help you listen to yourself better, and in their presence you will feel safe and able to be open and honest with yourself. That way, you begin thinking authentically, and when you do that you begin making the best decisions you can for yourself.

There are three main types of psychological therapy:[2]

Person-centred therapy This is the therapy originally developed by Carl Rogers and which is specifically developed to help people become more authentic. The therapist offers a supportive and empathic unconditionally regarding relationship in which you can think about yourself and your situation, and work out what steps to take next. This is the type of therapy that is best designed to help you live authentically.

Psychodynamic therapy This form of therapy is based on the principles first developed by Sigmund Freud about how unconscious processes need to be brought into awareness. Problems are often thought to have their roots in childhood events that have been forgotten. By helping you to understand your defence processes you will be able to confront issues more realistically.

Cognitive-behavioural therapy This form of therapy is based on writers such as Aaron Beck and Albert Ellis and is often used to help people understand when they fall into thinking traps, such as catastrophic thinking, or overgeneralising. Such thinking traps are related to various problems in living, so helping people recognise when they fall into these traps can aid them in combating feelings of depression and anxiety.

The above are snapshot descriptions but they should give you a flavour of each, which will be useful if you decide to seek professional help.

These varied forms of therapy have their different appeal and all can be helpful. What makes person-centred therapy stand out from the other two, however, and why it is more in keeping with the themes of this book, is that it is about helping people live to their fullest potential. It sees the problems that people have in living as arising when their potential has become thwarted in some way. This is an important point because, seen this way, therapy is not about treating a condition but it is about a process of self-discovery.

In the UK, the main organisations are:

British Psychological Society (BPS)
The BPS maintains a register of psychotherapists and coaching psychologists.
Website: http://www.bps.org.uk/psychology-publicfind-psychologist/find-psychologist

Health Care Professional Council (HCPC)
All practitioner psychologists have to be registered with the HCPC if they describe themselves as a clinical psychologist or as a counselling psychologist.
Website: http://www.hcpc-uk.co.uk/aboutregistration/professions/index.asp?id=14

British Association for Counselling and Psychotherapy (BACP)
The BACP are the largest body specialising in counselling and psychotherapy.
Website: http://www.itsgoodtotalk.org.uk/therapists

Meeting with a therapist can be helpful, but like any other meeting between two people, if you don't feel that you click with the other person in some way, then it might be difficult. The reason I say this is because often it takes trust to be built up before people feel genuinely safe with a therapist so that they are comfortable and able to talk openly about their deepest fears, guilt, shame or sadness. Don't worry, then, if you meet one or two before you settle on someone you want to work with. Ask questions about their background, qualifications and their approach to therapy. Good therapists will be pleased to talk to you about what they do and why they do it. They will answer all your questions and put you at ease. They won't expect you to do anything you don't want to do or talk about anything you feel uncomfortable with. Beware anyone who uses a lot of jargon or if they don't seem to notice if you are not following what they are saying. Of course, if you shop around for too long, you need to ask yourself if you are avoiding getting on with it for some reason.

Coaches and coaching psychologists

If you do not feel that you have significant problems that demand the attention of a psychological therapist but you are curious about learning about yourself and finding more authentic ways of living, you might find it useful to meet a coach or coaching psychologist. These are professionals who help people develop their character strengths and other capacities for personal and professional development. A coach can help you set goals and make commitments to new actions, whether it be in your personal or professional life. Life coaches help people think through new directions in their personal lives. Business coaches, or executive coaches, will help you develop your leadership skills and function more effectively in your work.

Further Reading

The following are some books that I think are worth reading to deepen your understanding of some of the issues I have talked about.

Carl Rogers's life and work

Rogers, C. R. (1980), *A Way of Being*, Boston: Houghton Mifflin

This is one of his later books and is a collection of his writings that cover his career from the 1960s onwards. He writes about his personal and professional experiences, as well as person-centred ideas and their application to education.

Rogers, C. R. (1961), *On Becoming a Person*, Boston: Houghton Mifflin

This book has been reprinted many times and is probably the most well known of all Rogers's books. It is a good source of the main ideas behind his approach to therapy.

Positive psychology

Ben-Shahar, T. (2008), *Happier*, New York: McGraw Hill

This is a popular book on happiness that covers the main ideas of the positive psychologists. It is easy to read and full of practical tips.

Critical psychiatry

Bentall, R. (2010), *Doctoring the Mind: Why Psychiatric Treatments Fail*, London: Penguin

Written by one of the leading clinical psychologists, this book explores, questions and challenges how we think about mental illness.

General self-help

Jeffers, S. (2007), *Feel the Fear and do it Anyway*, London: Vermilion

One of the best and most popular self-help books ever written, this book offers some timeless wisdom for facing life's challenges.

Advice on dealing with adversity and trauma

Joseph, S. (2013), *What Doesn't Kill Us: A Guide to Overcoming Adversity and Moving Forward*, London: Piatkus

With practical exercises to try, this book challenges us to understand that adversity need not be the road to a damaged life but can be a springboard to a more purposeful one.

Preface

1   *Hamlet,* act I, scene iii, 78–80. The quote can be interpreted differently, but this is how it is most often understood and used

2   Authenticity has received little empirical research until recently. In 2002, Susan Harter, one of the most eminent psychologists and an expert on the topic, commented that 'there is no single, coherent body of literature on authentic self-behavior, no bedrock of knowledge' (p.382). See, Harter, S. (2002), 'Authenticity', in C.R. Snyder and S.J. Lopez (eds), *Handbook of Positive Psychology* (pp. 382–94), New York: Oxford University Press

3   See, Schmid, P.F. (2005). 'Authenticity and alienation: Towards an understanding of the person beyond the categories of order and disorder', in S. Joseph and R. Worsley (eds,). *Person-centred Psychopathology: A positive psychology of mental health* (pp. 75–90), Ross-on-Wye: PCCS books.

4   Rogers, C.R. (1961), *On Becoming a Person*, Boston, MA: Houghton Mifflin

5   Joseph, S. and Lewis, C. (1998), 'The Depression–Happiness Scale: Reliability and validity of a bipolar self-report scale', *Journal of Clinical Psychology*, 54, 537–44

6   Alex has gone on to become a leading positive psychologist and was the founder of the Centre for Applied Positive Psychology (CAPP) http://www.cappeu.com/About

7   Wood, A.M., Linley, P.A., Maltby, J., Baliousis, M., and Joseph, S. (2008), 'The authentic personality: A theoretical and empirical conceptualization and the development of the authenticity scale', *Journal*

of Counselling Psychology, 55, 385–99. The questionnaire is shown in Chapter 7

8   The term post-traumatic growth was originally coined in the mid-1990s by two American clinical researchers, Lawrence Calhoun and Richard Tedeschi

9   As noted on pp. 134–5, Joseph, S. (2011), *What Doesn't Kill Us: The New Psychology Of Posttraumatic Growth*, New York: Basic Books

10   http://bronnieware.com/regrets-of-the-dying/

11   And research also shows that trauma work can be growthful for therapists, see: Linley, P.A., Joseph, S. and Loumidis, K. (2005), 'Trauma work, sense of coherence, and positive and negative changes in therapists', *Psychotherapy and Psychosomatics*, 74, 185–8

Chapter 1

1   As reported in *Independent* I, Wednesday 15 July, 2005, p. 25

2   Often attributed to Dr Seuss but not clear that he actually originated it: see, https://en.wikiquote.org/wiki/Dr._Seuss

3   Carl Rogers proposed that internal conflict – incongruence – leads to psychological tension, which can manifest itself in a number of ways, and always unique to the person. Similarly, cognitive dissonance is the term introduced by Leon Festinger. See, Festinger, L. (1957), *A Theory of Cognitive Dissonance*, Stanford, CA: Stanford University Press. We feel compelled to reduce the feeling of dissonance. More recently it has been proposed that inauthenticity is experienced by people as immoral, leading to the need to cleanse oneself: see: Gino, F., Kouchaki, M. and Galinsky, A.D. (2015), 'The moral virtue of authenticity: How inauthenticity produces feelings of immorality and impurity', *Psychological Science: Research, Theory, and Applications in Psychology and Related Sciences*, 26, 983–96.

4   See, Goffman, E. (1959), *The Presentation of Self in Everyday Life*

5   Wilber, K. (1979), *No Boundary: Eastern and Western Approaches to Personal Growth*, Boulder: Shambhala. In this book Wilber uses the analogy of riding a horse to describe how people often treat their bodies.

6   Taken from an edited extract of Steve Jobs's commencement address to students graduating from Stanford University in 2005 as reported in *Independent*, Friday 7 October, 2011

7   Aron, A. and Aron, E. (1989), *The Heart of Social Psychology*, 2nd edn, Lexington, MA: Lexington Books. See page 27

8   Asch, S.E. (1955, November), 'Opinions and social pressure', *Scientific American*, 31, 5

9   Vonk, R. (1998), 'The slime effect: Suspicion and dislike of likeable behavior toward superiors', *Journal of Personality and Social Psychology*, 74(4), 849

10   Teven, J. J. (2008), 'An examination of perceived credibility of the 2008 presidential candidates: Relationships with believability, like-ability, and deceptiveness', *Human Communication*, 11(4), 391–408

11   It is possible to feel authentic, but such feelings can be misleading and can be part of our self-deception. In one study, it was found that those who felt authentic when gambling reported behaviours associated with problem gambling. Lister, J.J. (2015), 'The dark side of authentic-ity: Feeling "real" while gambling interacts with enhancement motives to predict problematic gambling behaviour', *Journal of Gambling Studies*, 31, 995–1013

12   Thanks to my colleague Angela Smith – Dr Resilience – for this phrase

Part I

1   Olds, J. and Milner, P. (1954), 'Positive reinforcement produced by electrical stimulation of the septal area and other regions of rat brain', *Journal of Comparative and Physiological Psychology*, 47, 419–29

2   For discussions on the philosophy of hedonia and eudaimonia, see Nafstad, H. (2015), 'Historical, philosophical, and epistemological perspectives', in S. Joseph (ed.), *Positive Psychology in Practice: Promoting Human Flourishing in Work, Health, Education and Everyday Life*, Hoboken: Wiley. See also: Niemiec, C.P. and Ryan, R.M. (2013), 'What makes for a life well lived? Autonomy and its relation to full functioning and organismic wellness', in S.A. David., I. Boniwell and A. Conley-Ayers (eds), *The Oxford Handbook of Happiness* (pp. 214–26). And see also: Ryan, R.M., Huta, V. and Deci, E.L. (2008), 'Living well: A self-determination theory perspective on eudaimonia', *Journal of Happiness Studies*, 9, 139–70

3   As a young man, Aristotle left Macedonia for Athens where he studied at Plato's academy for the next 20 years. Seen as one of the greatest philosophers of his day, he was invited by King Phillip of Macedonia to tutor his son who was to be Alexander the Great. Subsequently, Aristotle returned to Athens where he opened his own academy, the 'Lyceum'.

4   Morgan, M.L. (2001), *Classics of Moral and Political Theory*, Cambridge, MA: Hackett Publishing Co. As cited in Nafsted, H. (2015), 'Historical, philosophical, and epistemological perspectives', in Joseph, S. (ed.), *Positive Psychology in Practice: Promoting Human Flourishing in Work, Health, Education and Everyday Life*. Hoboken: Wiley

5   See, Franklin, S.S. (2006), *The Psychology of Happiness: A Good Human Life*, Cambridge

6   A brief biography of Abraham Maslow: Maslow was born in Brooklyn, New York, in 1908 of Russian Jewish immigrant parents. The story goes that Abe, as he was known, was a bright but shy and lonely boy, so convinced of his ugliness that he would ride deserted subway cars

so that others would not have to see him. Perhaps because of this he chose to study psychology, attending City College of New York and then the University of Wisconsin before returning to New York where he worked and was later surrounded by many of the scholars who had fled Nazi Europe. After the war, in 1951 he moved to Boston to work at Brandeis University. Early in his career he was an enthusiastic adherent of Sigmund Freud's ideas, but over time came to see them as offering a lopsided view. Freud, the founder of psychoanalysis, was concerned with the causes of human neurosis. The solution was to seek to understand the person's unconscious mind. As a result, psychoanalysis was termed a 'depth psychology' because it required the exploration into the darkest and unchartered areas of a person. In contrast to Freud, who helped us understand so much about what goes wrong with people, Maslow was concerned with what went right. Freud had given us depth psychology, now it was over to Maslow who gave us 'height psychology'. For Maslow, psychoanalysis had relied too heavily on case studies of people who were dysfunctional. Instead, he strove to create a psychology based not only on those who were dysfunctional, but also upon those who were fully living the extent of their human potential. That is to say, unlike Freud who had studied those who were distressed and unhappy, Maslow studied those who were functioning well in life. In this way he was able to explore the best of the human experience. This was the start of the movement that would come to be designated as 'humanistic psychology'. It was over 50 years ago in 1963 when the American Association for Humanistic Psychology (AAHP) was formed

7   Although it is not certain that Maslow himself ever presented it as a pyramid. He used the term hierarchy of needs to convey the idea that only as some needs are satisfied can the person move to the next. Another way of thinking about it is like Russian dolls; each of the needs are nested within the previous need

8   See, Maslow, A.H. (1968), *Toward a Psychology of Being* (2nd edn), New York: Van Nostrand

9   Maslow, A.H. (1943), 'A theory of human motivation', *Psychological Review*, 50, 370–96. Reprinted as Chapter 2 in Maslow, A.H. (1987), *Motivation and Personality* (3rd edn), New York: Harper (p. 22)

10 Jones, A. and Crandall, R. (1986), 'Validation of a short index of self-actualization', *Personality and Social Psychology Bulletin*, 12, 63–76. This description of self-actualisation is derived from the statement on this questionnaire, which was devised to assess differences among people in the amount they have self-actualised. For example, research using the index has found that those who score high tend to be less materialistic and to have greater self-acceptance, see Chan, R. and Joseph, S. (2000). 'Dimensions of personality, domains of

aspiration, and subjective well-being', *Personality and Individual Differences*, 28, 347–354.

11 Maslow, A. H. (1969), 'The farther reaches of human nature', *Journal of Transpersonal Psychology*, 1, 1–9. See also Skelsey Guest, H. (2014), 'Maslow's hierarchy of needs: The sixth level', *Psychologist*, 27, 982–3

12 Maslow, A.H. (1970), *Motivation and Personality* (rev. edn), New York: Harper and Row (p. 176)

13 As quoted in Lowry, R. (1973), *A. H. Maslow: An Intellectual Portrait*, Monterey, CA: Brooks/Cole (p. 91)

14 The metaphor about gravity was provided by Tudor, K. and Worrall, M. (2006), *Person-centred Therapy: A Clinical Philosophy*, London Routledge

15 A brief biography of Karen Horney: Karen Horney was one of the first women in Germany to be admitted to medical school. By 1920 she was a leading figure in psychoanalytical circles, as a founding member of the Berlin Psychoanalytical Institute. In 1932 she moved to America where she first worked at the Chicago Psychoanalytical Institute and then the New York Psychoanalytical Institute; however, she found that psychoanalysis was too dominated by the male perspective and so started to develop new ideas. It was in Horney's book *Neurosis and Human Growth* that she made her greatest contribution and challenge to Freudian thinking about human nature

16 Horney, K. (1950), *Neurosis and Human Growth*, New York: Norton (pp. 15–16)

17 Rogers, C.R. (1963), 'The actualising tendency in relation to "motives" and to consciousness', in M. Jones (ed.), *Nebraska Symposium on Motivation*, vol. 11. Lincoln: University of Nebraska Press, (pp 1–24).

18 Rogers, C.R. (1980), *A Way of Being*, Boston: Houghton Mifflin (p. 118). See also B.E. Levitt (ed.) (2008), *Reflections on Human Potential: Bridging The Person-Centered Approach and Positive Psychology*, Ross-on-Wye: PCCS Books.

19 A brief biography of Carl Rogers: Born in 1902 in a suburb of Chicago, Rogers's upbringing was strict and guided by the strong Protestant Christian ethos of his parents who preached the necessity of hard work. The Rogers family was wary of others outside their immediate group who they saw as engaging in dubious and corrupt practices of smoking, drinking, dancing and other unmentionable activities, and so life was kept very much within the family unit. As a boy, Carl was lonely and somewhat sickly and sought solace in his books. In 1914 the family moved to a large farm, which further isolated the young Carl from the outside world. 'I realized by now that I was peculiar, a loner, with very little place or opportunity for a place in the world of persons. I was socially incompetent in any but superficial contacts.' Quoted from, Rogers, C.R. (1973), 'My philosophy of interpersonal

relationships and how it grew', *Journal of Humanistic Psychology*, 13, 3–16 (p. 4). Living on the farm, Rogers became fascinated by the wildlife around him, becoming knowledgeable about night-flying moths, which inhabited the local woods, and began to breed them in captivity. He studied their life cycle and observed the cocoons during the long winter months. In the 1940s and 1950s the fashion in psychology was to look at people as if they were machines, purely shaped by the levers of reinforcement like the rats in the famous Skinner boxes, or conditioned by environmental events as with Pavlov's dogs. It was not surprising that Rogers, with his background growing up on the farm, took a different view. Rogers's view was that all life, including human life, is driven by a tendency towards realising its potential. Today, Rogers is best remembered for his books, *Client-Centered Therapy: Its Current Practice, Implications and Theory*, published in 1951, and '*On Becoming a Person: A Therapist's View of Psychotherapy*, published in 1961, both of which have been reprinted numerous times and remain in print and widely read. At one point he served as the president of the American Psychological Association, and towards the end of his life he was even nominated for the Nobel Peace Prize for his contributions to conflict reduction. Rogers was one of the most influential psychologists of the 20th century and the founder of a form of counselling and psychotherapy known as the 'person-centred approach'.For a full biography of Rogers, see Thorne, B. (1992), *Carl Rogers*, London: Sage. And see, Kirschenbaum, H. (2007), *The Life and Work of Carl Rogers*, Ross-on-Wye: PCCS Books

20   See Joseph, S. and Worsley, R. (eds), (2005), *Person-centred Psychopathology: Positive Psychological Perspectives on Mental Health*, Ross-on-Wye: PCCS Books. This book looks at the clinical applications of Carl Rogers's ideas to the different problems in living that people have

21   See also Ryan, R.M. and Deci, E.L (2000), 'The darker and brighter sides of human existence: Basic psychological needs as a unifying concept', *Psychological Inquiry*, 11, 319–38. These researchers, in the tradition of Carl Rogers, put forward the view that the thwarting of people's basic needs helps us understand why problems in living result

22   Psychiatrists have tried to classify personality disorders into categories such as borderline personality disorder, narcissistic personality disorder and psychopathic personality disorder, but the lines between these categories is hard to define. From the point of view of Rogers's theory of personality development, while there may be commonalities how each person becomes thwarted and twisted in the actualisation of their potential is unique to them

23 In psychology, the idea that people are striving toward their potential is an idea most associated with Carl Rogers, one of the pioneers
of humanistic psychology in the 1950s. His philosophy was that all
biological life has an inherent tendency to realise itself. Rogers used
the term 'actualisation' to mean a directional tendency – which, as
we will see, can result in positive or negative outcomes. See, Rogers,
C.R. (1963), 'Actualising tendency in relation to "Motives" and to consciousness', in M. Jones (ed), *Nebraska Symposium on motivation,
Vol. 11* Lincoln: University of Nebraska Press, (pp. 1-24). The idea is
that there is a tendency towards growth – it is not a guarantee of full
health and well-being – what is actualised depends on the environment. One other notable scholar and therapist who took this view was
Karen Horney in her famous book *Neurosis and Human Growth*

24 James, W. (1890/1983), *Principles of Psychology*, with introduction by
George A. Miller. Cambridge, MA: Harvard University Press, (p. 488)

25 One exception is the chimpanzee, which typically grooms itself when
given a mirror, see Gallup, G.G. (1979), 'Self-awareness in primates',
American Scientist, 67, 417–21

26 Lewis, M. and Brooks-Gunn, J. (1979), *Social Cognition and The
Acquisition Of Self*, New York: Plenum

27 Since Carl Rogers, others have developed similar theoretical
perspectives, notably Richard Ryan and Edward Deci, whose Self-
Determination Theory (SDT) says that people have basic needs
for autonomy, relatedness and competence, and that when these
needs are met, people will flourish. The terminology is different but
the ideas are strikingly similar. Interested readers can explore the
similarities between the two theories in Patterson, T. and Joseph,
S. (2007), 'Person-centered personality theory: Support from self-
determination theory and positive psychology', *Journal of Humanistic
Psychology*, 47, 117–39. See also Joseph, S. (2015), *Positive Therapy:
Building Bridges Between Positive Psychology and Person-Centred
Psychotherapy*, London: Routledge. Research in the SDT tradition
talks about controlling parenting rather than conditional parenting.
The evidence is that controlling parenting thwarts the basic needs of
children. See for example Soenens, B., Park, S.Y., Vansteenkiste, M.
and Mouratidis, A. (2012), 'Perceived parental psychological control
and adolescent depressive experiences: A cross-cultural study with
Belgian and South-Korean adolescents', *Journal of Adolescence*, 35,
261–72

28 See Wilkins, P. (2005), 'Person-centred theory and mental illness', in
S. Joseph and R. Worsley (eds), *Person-centred psychopathology: A
positive psychology of mental health*. Ross-on-Wye: PCCS Books. In
this chapter Wilkins summarises Rogers's theory of child development

29   Rogers, C.R. (1973), 'My philosophy of interpersonal relationships and how it grew', *Journal of Humanistic Psychology*, 13, 3–16 (p. 13)

30   *Tao Te Ching: The Book of the Way*, translated by Stephen Mitchell (2000), London: Macmillan. We don't know much about Lao-tzu. His name translates as the 'Old Master'. Possibly he was a contemporary of Confucius. In fact, we are not even sure he existed, but within his book is one of the most influential philosophies on the art of living and on how to govern whether that of a child or a nation

31   Quoted in Rogers, C.R. (1973), 'My philosophy of interpersonal relationships and how it grew', *Journal of Humanistic Psychology*, 13, 3–16 (p. 13)

32   As already noted above, Richard Ryan and Edward Deci and their colleagues have developed an extensive body of research knowledge, supporting the view that human flourishing arises when basic needs are supported. To find out more, their work can be seen in more detail at: http://www.selfdeterminationtheory.org/

33   Nix, G.A., Ryan, R.M., Manly, J.B. and Deci, E.L. (1999), 'Revitalisation through self-regulation: The effects of autonomous and controlled motivation on happiness and vitality', *Journal of Experimental Social Psychology*, 35, 266–84

34   Huta, V. (2012), 'Linking people's pursuit of eudaimonia and hedonia with characteristics of their parents: Parenting styles, verbally endorsed values, and role modelling', *Journal of Happiness Studies*, 13, 47–61. This study shows that parents who model eudaimonia had children who grew up to derive well-being from eudaimonic and hedonic pursuits, whereas parents who role-modelled hedonia had children who grew up to derive well-being only from hedonia

35   Assor, A., Roth, G. and Deci, E.L. (2004), 'The emotional costs of parents' conditional regard: A self-determination theory analysis', *Journal of Personality*, 72, 47–88

36   These items are based on those used by Assor and colleagues; the interested reader is advised to consult the original article for the actual items

37   See also, Roth, G. and Assor, A. (2010), 'Parental conditional regard as a predictor of deficiencies in young children's capacities to respond to sad feelings', *Infant and Child Development*, 19, 465–77. In this study it was found that parents' use of conditional regard can promote suppression of children's feelings; for example, parents who themselves are uncomfortable with their own emotions are then positively regarding of their children when they similarly react unemotionally, or withdraw their affection for their children when they see them reacting emotionally. What the researchers found was that, as a result, children lack skills in recognising emotions of sadness in others and

lack an awareness of sadness in themselves. For more information on the work of Avi Assor, see also: http://www.selfdeterminationtheory.org/authors/avi-assor/

38 Mruk, C. J. (2015), 'Self-esteem, relationships and positive psychology: Concepts, research and connections', in M. Hojjat and D. Cramer (eds), *Positive Psychology of Love*, New York: Oxford University Press, (pp. 149–61)

39 Maslow, A.H. (1971), *Farther Reaches of Human Nature*, New York: Penguin, Arkana (pp. 44–5)

40 For a discussion, see Sanders, P. and Hill, A. (2014), *Counselling for Depression: A Person-Centred and Experiential Approach to Practice*, London: Sage

41 We seek to find consistency between our experiences and our self-concept. Typically, people maintain their self-concept with a process of defence, see Rogers, C. R. (1959), 'A theory of therapy, personality and interpersonal relationships, as developed in the client-centered framework', In S. Koch (ed), *Psychology: A study of a science*, (3): Formulations of the person and the social context, 184–256, New York: McGraw-Hill

42 For a more comprehensive overview of research on relationships and well-being, see Cooper, M. and Joseph, S. (2016), 'Psychological foundations for humanistic psychotherapeutic practice', in D.J. Cain, K. Keenan and S. Rubin (eds), *Humanistic Psychotherapies: Handbook of Research and Practice*, Washington, DC: American Psychological Association (pp. 11–46)

43 For a review of research showing that more empathic, genuine and unconditionally regarding therapy relationships are helpful to people, see Murphy, D. and Joseph, S. (2016), 'Person-centered therapy: Past, present and future orientations', in D.J. Cain, K. Keenan and S. Rubin (eds), *Humanistic Psychotherapies: Handbook of Research and Practice*, Washington, DC: American Psychological Association (pp. 185–218)

44 A brief biography of Sigmund Freud: Writing around the turn of the twentieth century, it was Freud who first took seriously the idea that our psychological difficulties have their roots in unconscious processes. He believed that people's behaviour was determined to a large extent by underlying psychological forces shaped through past experiences of which the person was not consciously aware. His greatest contribution was showing us that our mental world is governed by rules and a cause-effect structure. Freud's views exploded throughout Victorian society challenging traditional beliefs about culture, religion and sexuality. Freud developed psychoanalysis, which was a form of psychological treatment that helped people explore their

unconscious and come to terms with the conflicts they discovered. Because the psychoanalyst was digging deep into the unconscious mind of his or her patients, this approach was referred to as a 'depth psychology'. Freud's ideas were at first greeted with some scepticism by the medical community of the time, but following his visit to the United States in 1909 to present a series of lectures at Clark University in Worcester, Massachusetts, he won over the American psychological community becoming the most influential psychological theorist in the Western world. In all, Freud wrote 24 volumes on psychoanalytical theory, which are still on the bookshelves of therapists today. Following the Nazi annexation of Austria in 1938 Freud, at the age of 82, relocated to London where he died 18 months later in 1939, in the first few weeks of World War II. His books were burned by Nazis but Freud famously said, 'What progress we are making. In the Middle Ages they would have burnt me, nowadays they are content with burning my books.' Freud was of course not to know at that time that the Nazis would indeed have been content to burn him too if they had had the chance. In his last years he suffered from ill health and cancer of the mouth and jaws. Visitors today to his home in London's Hampstead, which is now a museum dedicated to his life and work, can see copies of his original manuscripts, psychoanalytic couch, and his study preserved as it was in his lifetime. Perhaps Sigmund Freud's biggest contribution was his claim that the 'child is father to the man'. What he meant was that early life experiences play a formative role in personality development. For many, an image of the psychology profession is that of someone lying on a coach talking about their childhood. Many of the ideas of Freud seem out of place in the modern world, but the key idea that we are shaped by what happens to us in childhood is now accepted by most psychologists. Since Freud, looking back at how our early experiences has shaped us is a common pursuit among psychologists and psychotherapists, although not many have their clients lie on couches today

45   The following list of defence mechanisms is not meant to be comprehensive or reflect any particular theory, although I have been influenced by the Defence Style Questionnaire as a guide to whether the mechanism is best considered mature or immature. See Andrews, G., Singh, M., and Bond, M. (1993), 'The Defence Style Questionnaire', *Journal of Nervous and Mental Disease*, 181(4), 246–56

46   Also, research has found that those with a diagnosis of psychosis are more likely to use immature defences, see Bond, M.P. and Sagala Vaillant, J. (1986), 'An empirical study of the relationship between diagnosis and defence style', *Archives of General Psychiatry*, 43, 285–8

47 Joseph, S. (2013), *What Doesn't Kill Us: A Guide to Overcoming Adversity and Moving Forward*, London: Piatkus
48 Taylor, S. and Brown, J.D. (1988), 'Illusion and well-being: A social psychological perspective on mental health', *Psychological Bulletin*, 103, 193–210. In this paper the authors make the case for the protective and health-related benefits of self-deception
49 'Unbiased processing' is the term used by Michael Kernis and Brian Goldman at the University of Georgia to refer to our ability to be objective to self-relevant information

Part II

1 Seligman, M.E.P. (2004), Foreword, in P.A. Linley and S. Joseph (eds), *Positive Psychology in Practice*, Hoboken: Wiley (pp. xi–xiii)
2 Now there are courses in universities about happiness, magazine articles and lots of books by psychologists on happiness. Happiness is now a respected field of study. Indeed, in 2013, Oxford University Press published a book entitled the *Oxford Handbook of Happiness*, which is a landmark collection of 79 chapters written by the world's leading experts. For the more practical applications, see Joseph, S. (2015), *Positive Psychology in Practice: Promoting Human Flourishing in Work, Health, Education and Everyday Life* (2nd edition), Hoboken: Wiley
3 Positive psychology is often characterised as the study of the hedonic life. In its earliest years there was indeed too much emphasis on the pursuit of pleasure, but interest has now turned to the eudaimonic life. Positive psychologists understand that, ultimately, happiness depends on getting the right balance between pleasure and purpose
4 See, Robbins, B.D. (2015), 'Building bridges between humanistic and positive psychology', in S. Joseph (ed.), *Positive Psychology in Practice: Promoting Human Flourishing in Work, Health, Education and Everyday Life*, Hoboken: Wiley
5 Rogers, C.R. (1961), *On Becoming a Person*, Boston, MA: Houghton Mifflin, (pp. 186–7)
6 These directions are listed in Rogers, C.R. (1961), *On Becoming a Person*, Boston, MA: Houghton Mifflin
7 Huta, V. (2015), 'Eudaimonia and hedonia: Their complementary functions in life and how they can be pursued in practice', in S. Joseph (ed.), *Positive Psychology in Practice: Promoting Human Flourishing in Work, Health, Education and Everyday Life* (2nd edn), Hoboken: Wiley. For more information about Veronika Huta's work see her home page: http://veronikahuta.weebly.com/
8 Fredrickson, B. L., Grewen, K. M., Coffey, K. A., Algoe, S. B., Firestine, A. M., Arevalo, J. M., and Cole, S. W. (2013), 'A functional genomic

perspective on human well-being', *Proceedings of the National Academy of Sciences*, 110(33), 13684–89

9   Steger, M.F., Kashdan, T.B. and Oishi, S. (2008), 'Being good by doing good: Daily eudaimonic activity and well-being', *Journal of Research in Personality*, 42, 22–42

10 Huta, V. and Ryan, R.M. (2010), 'Pursuing pleasure or virtue: The differential and overlapping well-being benefits of hedonic and eudaimonic motives', *Journal of Happiness Studies*, 11, 735–62

11 Wood, A.M and Joseph, S. (2010), 'The absence of positive psychological (eudemonic) well-being as a risk factor for depression: A ten year cohort study', *Journal of Affective Disorders*, 12, 213–17

12 See, Kasser, T. (2002), *The High Price Of Materialism*, Cambridge, MA: MIT Press. See also, Kasser, T. (2015), 'The science of values in the culture of consumption', in S. Joseph (ed.), *Positive Psychology in Practice: Promoting Human Flourishing in Work, Health, Education and Everyday Life*, Hoboken: Wiley

13 As proposed in the Self-Determination Theory (SDT) developed by Ed Deci and Richard Ryan. See also the Self-Concordance Model developed by Ken Sheldon. The Self-Concordance Model suggests that the extent to which goal satisfaction results in positive well-being depends on whether a goal is self-concordant. Self-concordant goals derive from intrinsic motives that originate in inherent basic psychological needs. Attainment of these goals is more likely, as individuals invest sustained effort in pursuing them. In one study, Sheldon and Eliot conducted a longitudinal study among university students. In the beginning of the semester, students reported eight goals they had set for themselves and their motivation to pursue each goal. Three times throughout the semester, respondents reported the amount of effort put in pursuing each goal and the extent of attainment of that goal. Students put more effort in pursuing goals and were more successful in attaining them the more they were self-concordant. Goal attainment led to an experience of psychological need satisfaction, which correlated with improvement in well-being. See, Sheldon, K.M. and Elliot, A.J. (1999), 'Goal striving, need satisfaction and longitudinal well-being: The self-concordance model', *Journal of Personality and Social Psychology*, 76(3), 482

14 Sheldon, K.M. and Krieger, L.S. (2014), 'Walking the talk: Value importance, value enactment and well-being', *Motivation and Emotion*, published online.

15 Martin E.P. Seligman (2003), *Authentic Happiness: Using the New Positive Psychology to Realise Your Potential for Lasting Fulfilment*, London: Nicholas Brealey, p. 160

16 Adapted from Peterson, C. and Park, N. (2004), 'Classification and

measurement of character strengths: Implications for practice', in P.A. Linley and S. Joseph (eds), *Positive Psychology in Practice*, Hoboken: Wiley: (pp. 433-446)

17 Csikszentmihalyi, M. (2009), 'Flow', in S. Lopez (ed.), *The Encyclopedia of Positive Psychology* Hoboken: Wiley (pp. 394–400)

18 As already noted, the topic of authenticity received little empirical research prior to 2002. Since then it has become the focus of much new research by personality, development and positive psychologists. For a scholarly overview: see Harter, (2012), *The Construction of the Self: Developmental and Sociocultural Foundations* (2nd edn), New York: The Guilford Press

19 Wood, A.M., Linley, P.A., Maltby, J., Baliousis, M. and Joseph, S. (2008), 'The authentic personality: A theoretical and empirical conceptualisation and the development of the authenticity scale', *Journal of Counselling Psychology*, 55, 385–99. The questionnaire itself was based on the work of Carl Rogers and his theory of congruence. See, Barrett-Lennard, G.T. (1998), *Carl Rogers' Helping System: Journey and Substance*, London: Sage. The three components of the authenticity scale were derived through factor analysis. I refer to the three components here as knowing yourself, owning yourself and being yourself, but the corresponding technical terms used in the paper to describe these three components were self-alienation, accepting external influence and authentic living, respectively. The scale has been adapted for use in different contexts and countries. It was adapted for use in a work-related context: Van den Bosch, R. and Taris, T.W. (2014), 'Authenticity at work: Development and validation of an individual authenticity measure at work', *Journal of Happiness Studies*, 15. Adapted for use in France: Gregoire, S., Baron, L., Menard, J. and Lachance, L. (2014), 'The Authenticity Scale: Psychometric properties of a French translation and exploration of its relationships with personality and well-being', *Canadian Journal of Behavioural Science*, 40, 346–55. Turkey: Satici, S.A., Kayis, A.R. and Akin, A. (2013), 'Predictive role of authenticity on psychological vulnerability in Turkish university students', *Psychological Reports*, 112, 519–28. Brazil: de Carvalho Chinelato, R.S., Ferreira, M.C. and Van den Bosch, R. (2015), 'Construct validity evidence for the individual authenticity measure at work in Brazilian samples', *Journal of Work and Organisational Psychology*.

20 Another measure is the Authenticity Inventory (AI) developed by Kernis and Goldman. This is a 46-item questionnaire, grouped into four scales: (1) awareness of oneself (e.g., 'I am often confused about my feelings'); (2) unbiased processing of information relevant

to ourselves (e.g., 'I find it very difficult to critically assess myself');
(3) behaviour (e.g., 'I am willing to change myself for others if the
reward is desirable enough'); (4) relations with others (e.g., 'I make
it a point to express to people who are close to me how much I truly
care for them'). For each item respondents are asked to say how
much they agree on a five-point scale ranging from 1 = strongly
disagree to 5 = strongly agree. See Kernis, M.H. and Goldman,
B.M. (2006), 'A multicomponent conceptualisation of authenticity:
Theory and research', in M.P. Zanna (ed.), *Advances in Experimental
Social Psychology*, vol. 38, San Diego, CA: Elsevier Academic Press
(pp. 283–357)

21   Lenton, A.P., Bruder, M., Slabu, L. and Sedikides, C. (2013), 'How
does "being real" feel? The experience of state authenticity', *Journal
of Personality*, 81, 276–89

22   Studies show that, on average, people who scored higher on tests for
authenticity are more satisfied with life, higher in self-esteem, less
depressed and anxious and more alert and awake. They also have
less physical symptoms such as headaches, aches and pains: e.g.,
Goldman, B. M. (2006), 'Making diamonds out of coal: The role
of authenticity in healthy (optimal) self-esteem and psychological
functioning', in M.H. Kernis (ed.), *Self-Esteem: Issues and Answers*,
New York: Psychology Press (pp. 132–19). See also, Kernis, M.H.
and Goldman, B.M. (2006), 'A multicomponent conceptualisation
of authenticity: Theory and research', in M.P. Zanna (ed.), *Advances
in Experimental Social Psychology*, vol. 38, San Diego, CA: Elsevier
Academic Press (pp. 283–357); Lakey, C.E., Kernis, M.H., Heppner,
W.L. and Lance, C.E. (2008), 'Individual differences in authenticity
and mindfulness as predictors of verbal defensiveness', *Journal of
Research in Personality*, 42, 230–8; Wood, A.M., Linley, P.A., Maltby,
J., Baliousis, M. and Joseph, S. (2008), 'The authentic personality: A
theoretical and empirical conceptualisation and the development of
the authenticity scale', *Journal of Counselling Psychology*, 55, 385–99.
Gregoire, S., Baron, L., Menard, J. and Lachance, L. (2014), 'The
Authenticity Scale: Psychometric properties of a French translation
and exploration of its relationships with personality and well-being',
Canadian Journal of Behavioural Science, 40, 346–55; Vainio, M. M.
and Daukantaitė, D. (2015), 'Grit and different aspects of well-being:
Direct and indirect relationships via sense of coherence and authenticity', *Journal of Happiness Studies*. Published online DOI 10.1007/
s10902-015-9688-7

23   Lenton, A.P., Bruder, M., Slabu, L. and Sedikides, C. (2013). 'How
does "being real" feel? The experience of state authenticity', *Journal
of Personality*, 81, 276–89

24   Boyraz, G., Waits, J.B. and Felix, V.A. (2014), 'Authenticity, life satis-
     faction and distress: A longitudinal analysis', *Journal of Counselling
     Psychology*, 61, 498–505. This was a cross-lagged panel analysis
     showing that authenticity predicted distress and satisfaction, but the
     relationship was unidirectional as distress and satisfaction did not
     predict authenticity.

25   Kifer, Y., Heller, D., Perunovic, W.Q.E. and Galinsky, A.D. (2013), 'The
     good life of the powerful: The experience of power and authenticity
     enhances subjective well-being', *Psychological Science: Research,
     Theory, and Application in Psychology and Related Sciences*, 24,
     280–88

26   Harker, L. and Keltner, D. (2001), 'Expressions of positive emotion in
     women's college yearbook pictures and their relationship to person-
     ality and life outcomes across adulthood', *Journal of Personality and
     Social Psychology*, 80(1), 112. For other studies, see Harter, S. (2012),
     *The Construction of The Self: Developmental and Sociocultural
     Foundations* (2nd edn), New York: The Guilford Press

27   Bryan, J., Baker, Z. and Tou, R. (2015), 'Prevent the blue, be true to you:
     Authenticity buffers the negative impact of loneliness on alcohol-related
     problems, physical symptoms, and depressive and anxiety symptoms',
     Journal of Health Psychology ,DOI:10.1177/1359105315609090

28   One example is how authentic people tend to have a higher sense of
     coherence, which refers to their sense that the world and oneself are
     comprehensible, manageable, and meaningful. See, Vainio, M. M.
     and Daukantaitė D. (2015), 'Grit and different aspects of well-being:
     Direct and indirect relationships via sense of coherence and authen-
     ticity' *Journal of Happiness Studies*. Published online DOI 10.1007/
     s10902-015-9688-7.

29   See: Gino, F., Kouchaki, M. and Galinsky, A.D. (2015), 'The moral
     virtue of authenticity: How inauthenticity produces feelings of immo-
     rality and impurity', *Psychological Science: Research, Theory, and
     Applications in Psychology and Related Sciences*, 26, 983–96

30   Akin, A. and Akin, U. (2014), 'Examining the relationship between
     authenticity and self-handicapping', *Psychological Reports*, 115,
     795–804

31   Lakey, C.E., Kernis, M.H., Heppner, W.L. and Lance, C.E. (2008),
     'Individual differences in authenticity and mindfulness as predictors
     of verbal defensiveness', *Journal of Research in Personality*, 42(1),
     230–38

32   Schlegel, R.J., Hicks, J.A., Arndt, J. and King, L.A. (2009), 'Thine own
     self: True self-concept accessibility and meaning in life', *Journal of
     Personality and Social Psychology*, 96, 473–90

33   White, N.J. and Tracey, T.J.G. (2011), 'An examination of career

indecision and application to dispositional authenticity', *Journal of Vocational Behaviour*, 78, 219–24

34   Hirschorn, S. and Hefferon, K. (2013), 'Leaving it all behind to travel: Venturing uncertainty as a means to personal growth and authenticity', *Journal of Humanistic Psychology*, 53, 283–306

35   Vainio, M.M. and Daukantaitė, D. (2015), 'Grit and different aspects of well-being: Direct and indirect relationships via sense of coherence and authenticity', *Journal of Happiness Studies*. Published online DOI 10.1007/s10902-015-9688-7

36   As reported in Kernis, M.H. and Goldman, B.M. (2006), 'A multi-component conceptualisation of authenticity: Theory and research', *Advances in Experimental Social Psychology*, 38, 283–357

37   Pinto, D.G., Maltby, J., Wood, A.M. and Day, L. (2012), 'A behavioural test of Horney's linkage between authenticity and aggression: People living authentically are less-likely to respond aggressively in unfair situations', *Personality and Individual Differences*, 52 (1), 41–4

38   Perceiving authenticity in one's partner is related to relationship goals, interpersonal trust and relationship outcomes. Wickham, R.E. (2013), 'Authenticity in romantic partners', *Journal of Experimental Social Psychology*, 49, 878–87

39   Swann Jr., W.B., De La Ronde, C. and Hixon, J.G. (1994), 'Authenticity and positivity strivings in marriage and courtship', *Journal of Personality and Social Psychology*, 66, 857–69

40   See, Rodriguez, L.M., Knee, C.R. and Neighbors, C. (2013), 'Relationships can drive some to drink: Relationship-contingent self-esteem and drinking problems', *Journal of Social and Personal Relationships*, 31, 270–90

41   Neff, K.D. and Suizzo, M.A. (2006), 'Culture, power, authenticity and psychological well-being within romantic relationships: A comparison of European American and Mexican Americans', *Cognitive Development*, 21, 441–57

42   Lopez, F.G. and Rice, K.G. (2006), 'Preliminary development and validation of a measure of relationship authenticity', *Journal of Counselling Psychology*, 53, 362–71

Part III

1   A quote often attributed to Einstein but it seems it is not certain what the original source is: https://en.wikiquote.org/wiki/Talk:Albert_Einstein

2   Adapted from De Shazer, S. (1988), *Clues: Investigating solutions in brief therapy*, New York: Norton (p.78)

3   Based on, Leary, M.R. (1983), 'A brief version of the fear of negative

evaluation scale', *Personality and Social Psychology Bulletin*, 9(3), 371–6

4   Patterson, T. and Joseph, S. (2006), 'Development of a self-report measure of unconditional positive self-regard', *Psychology and Psychotherapy: Theory, Research and Practice*, 79, 557–70; Patterson, T.G. and Joseph, S. (2013), 'Unconditional Positive Self-Regard: A Person-centred approach to facilitating a non-contingent relationship with inner experiencing', in M.E. Berrnard (ed.), *The Strength of Self-acceptance: Theory, Practice and Research*, New York: Springer (pp. 93–106),

5   Oprah Winfrey (2014), 'What I know for sure', *Psychologies* Magazine, UK edition, p. 146

6   Story shared by Cathy Pover-Jones at Keele University and credited by her to Dr Frank Margison, consultant psychiatrist in psychotherapy, NWIDP Training Programme, 2004, Gaskell House Manchester.

7   Adapted from Sheldon, K. and Lyubomirsky, S. (2006), 'How to increase and sustain positive emotion: The effects of expressing gratitude and visualising best possible selves', *Journal of Positive Psychology*, 1(2), 73–82

Part IV

1   Dweck, C. (2006), *Mindset: The New Psychology of Success*, New York: Random House

2   As quoted by Damian Whitworth in his article about Peter Buffett in *The Times*, Thursday 10 April, 2014, pp. 4–5

3   For a recent review, Larson, R.W., and Dawes, N.P. (2015), 'Cultivating adolescents' motivation', in S. Joseph (ed.), *Positive Psychology in Practice: Promoting Human Flourishing in Work, Health, Education and Everyday Life*, Hoboken: Wiley (pp. 313–26)

4   Rogers, C. (1983), *Freedom to Learn for the 80s*, Columbus, OH: Charles Merrin (p. 120)

5   Sheldon, K.M., and Krieger, L.S. (2007), 'Understanding the negative effects of legal education on law students: A longitudinal test of self-determination theory', *Personality and Social Psychology Bulletin*, 33(6), 883–97

6   W. Timothy Gallwey (1986), *The Inner Game of Tennis*, London: Pan (p. 14), (first published in 1975)

7   Ibid. p. 24

8   Ibid. p. 28

9   Sivanathan, N., Arnold, K.A., Turner, N. and Barling, J. (2004), 'Leading well: Transformational leadership and well-being', in P.A. Linley and S. Joseph (eds), *Positive Psychology in Practice* (pp. 241–55), Hoboken: Wiley.

10 For an overview of the field, see Kauffman, C., Joseph, S. and
    Scoular, A. (2015), In S. Joseph (Ed.), *Positive Psychology in Practice:
    Promoting Human Flourishing in Work, Health, Education and
    Everyday Life*, Hoboken: Wiley

11 http://www.mind.org.uk/information-support/types-of-mental-
    health-problems/statistics-and-facts-about-mental-health/
    how-common-are-mental-health-problems/. For a discussion on
    prescription, diagnosis and mental health problems, see Sanders, P.
    and Hill, A. (2014), *Counselling for Depression: A Person-Centred and
    Experiential Approach to Practice*, London: Sage

12 http://www.mentalhealth.freeuk.com/article.htm

13 Bentall, R. (2010), *Doctoring the Mind: Why Psychiatric Treatments
    Fail*, London: Penguin. Quote taken from interview with Richard
    Bentall, *Psychologist*, 2011, vol. 24, p. 320, https://thepsychologist.
    bps.org.uk/volume-24/edition-4/one-onewith-richard-bentall

14 Schwartz, S.H. and Bardi, A. (2001), 'Value hierarchies across cul-
    tures: Taking a similarities perspective', *Journal of Cross-Cultural
    Psychology*, 32, 268–90

15 A survey of 573 users of 'Me2day' – a microblogging service in South
    Korea – found that those with a higher need for popularity were lower
    on authenticity than those with a lower need for popularity. The
    author of the report concludes that one's ability to be authentic may
    be increasingly challenged as we live our lives more publicly online.
    Lim, J.S. (2015), 'Online authenticity, popularity and the "real me" in
    a microblogging environment', *Computers in Human Behaviour*, 52,
    132–43. Other research shows that social network sites can, however,
    provide a forum for authenticity and users benefit in terms of their
    well-being from more authentic self-presentation: Reinecke, L. and
    Trepte, S. (2014), 'Authenticity and well-being on social network sites:
    A two-wave longitudinal study on the effects of online authenticity
    and the positivity bias in SNS communication', *Computers in Human
    Behaviour*, 30, 95–102

16 Wood, A.M. and Joseph, S. (2010), 'The absence of positive psycholog-
    ical (eudemonic) well-being as a risk factor for depression: A ten year
    cohort study', *Journal of Affective Disorders*, 12, 213–17

17 Peter Morrall discusses how therapy pays little attention to what is
    going on socially, how it can be a form of social control, and prevents
    sorting out problems for themselves, see Morrall, P. (2008), *The
    Trouble with therapy: Sociology and psychotherapy* Maidenhead:
    Open University. I've made the same point myself, see Joseph, S.
    (2007). 'Agents of social control?' *The Psychologist*, 20, 429–431.
    This may be true for many psychological therapies but possibly not
    for those therapies that strive to nurture authenticity. Carl Rogers

talked of the *quiet revolution* to describe the political agenda of how personal transformation leads to social change. As people change towards becoming more authentic, and they become more aware of their choices in life and choose to pursue a life dictated by their own values, they will, according to Rogers, move towards becoming more socially constructive in their behaviour, thus more active politically, more open to the suffering of others and more willing to engage at the social and political level. See Rogers, C.R. (1978), *Carl Rogers on Personal Power: Inner Strength and its Revolutionary Impact*, London: Constable

18 Chomsky, N. (2013), *On Anarchism*, London: Penguin (p. 33)

19 The idea of a happiness index was pioneered by the economist Sir Richard Layard and the positive psychologist Martin Seligman

20 Commissioned for a United Nations Conference on Happiness, the publication of the first 'World Happiness Report', edited by Jeffrey Sachs, Richard Layard and John Helliwell; as reported in the *Economist*, http://www.economist.com/blogs/feastandfamine/2012/04/happiness

21 Frankl was a psychiatrist in Vienna during the 1930s. He treated suicidal patients until the Nazi regime banned Jewish doctors from practising medicine. Then, in 1942, he was sent to the concentration camp of Theresienstadt with his wife and parents. The family was divided when his wife was transported to Bergen-Belsen and he and his parents sent to Auschwitz. By the time of liberation in 1945, Frankl had lost all his family. He alone had survived the Nazi extermination camps. After the war, Frankl served as a professor of psychiatry at the University of Vienna and as a visiting professor at Harvard University. Through his experiences and his clinical work, Frankl wrote one of the most important psychology books of the 20th century, *Man's Search for Meaning*, in which he describes his own experiences in the Nazi camps. Frankl emphasised the importance of how we choose to live our lives, and that despite whatever adversity befalls us, it is up to us alone to determine how we respond.

22 Frankl, V. (1985), *Man's Search For Meaning*, New York: Washington Square Press (p. 162). This book was originally published in 1946.

Appendices

1 See, Joseph, S. and Maltby, J. (2014), 'The Positive Functioning Inventory: Initial validation of a 12-item self-report measure of well-being', *Psychology of Well-Being: Theory, Research and Practice*, 4, 15.

2 See, Joseph, S. (2010), *Theories of Counselling and Psychotherapy: An introduction to the different approaches*, Basingstoke: Palgrave Macmillan

Index

(page numbers in *italics* refer to illustrations)